FRANK GIFFORD
THE GOLDEN YEAR 1956

MURRAY
OLDERMAN
16

FRANK GIFFORD

The Golden Year 1956

by William N. Wallace

Prentice-Hall, Inc., Englewood Cliffs, New Jersey

FRANK GIFFORD—THE GOLDEN YEAR 1956
by William N. Wallace

Library of Congress Catalog Card Number: 73-80768

Printed in the United States of America • *T*

13-331074-4

Prentice-Hall International, Inc., London
Prentice-Hall of Australia, Pty. Ltd., Sydney
Prentice-Hall of Canada, Ltd., Toronto
Prentice-Hall of India Private Ltd., New Delhi
Prentice-Hall of Japan, Inc., Tokyo

FOREWORD

In my fifteen years of coaching in the National Football League, I have been associated with many fine football players, but among them there have been only a half dozen I would be willing to acclaim as great. Frank Gifford was one of those.

Frank Gifford and I first met fifteen years ago, when I came to the New York Giants as an assistant coach and he was a second year back. He had been a great runner and a fine passer at the University of Southern California and, as you will read in this book, it was to make use of those two talents of his that I first put in the optional run-or-pass play that worked so well for the Giants and, later, for the Green Bay Packers, with Paul Hornung, another great player, in Frank Gifford's role.

It was also Frank Gifford who made our belly play

go, dipping his run to the outside when the defensive end would pinch in to prevent the pulling guard from blocking him out. Off this—the adjustments the other teams would make to cover that threat to the outside—we were able to free our flanker as a deep sideline receiver, and thus was born another play that has been a part of the repertoire of my teams ever since.

That is the origin of my appreciation of Frank Gifford, but it is by no means the whole of it. Frank Gifford was born with great talent, gifts that a lesser man, and a lesser athlete, might have taken for granted. Frank Gifford, however, seemed to realize that talent is, indeed, a gift, and that with that gift goes a moral responsibility—the moral responsibility of the recipient to perfect that gift, that talent, to the utmost. It was never enough for Frank Gifford to be good. He had to be better, and all of us who were a part of those Giant teams with him were better for that resolution, that determination.

The theme of this book exemplifies Frank Gifford's great pride and his perfectionist attitude. It exemplifies, too, what football is—the laughter and exhilaration when you win, and the shock and sadness when you lose that reflects, that is, in fact, life.

As must be obvious, I shall always have a lasting respect and admiration for Frank Gifford.

Vince Lombardi

Washington, D. C.

INTRODUCTION

The phone call that December morning in 1956 woke Frank Gifford.

"I've just finished counting up the votes for the Jim Thorpe Trophy," I told him over the phone.

"Huh?" Frank was still groggy from sleep.

"You know, for the most valuable player in the NFL. The players around the league have just voted for you."

"Hey, that's great," he said. Now he was up, and bright. He was at the Excelsior Hotel in mid-Manhattan, where he lived with Maxine and their three children during the football season. The call gave the kids an excuse to come in and romp with Daddy in the little studio bedroom.

Only the year before, a newspaper syndicate, NEA, had instituted the MVP award for pro football. And now Frank Gifford, who led the New York Giants to the National Football League championship in that year of 1956, was receiving the ultimate tribute from his peers.

"Everything good that's happened to me," Frank later reflected, "started from there." He meant from a career standpoint, because handsome Frank had already been the all-America campus hero, good-looking enough to act in pictures, and had married the campus queen. But basically, he was still a shy, withdrawn young man from Bakersfield, California, whose main talent was the ability to do things with a football. After his Golden Year of 1956, he burgeoned as a personality, too, and today we have Frank Gifford, still handsome, still a little shy, but also a poised personality whose annual income tallies in six figures for his sharp, smooth sports commentaries via television and radio.

It shows what one big year can do for a man—recognition and, in the case of Gifford, the acuity to make it an extension of his career when the zap went out of his muscles and he no longer could play football.

Through this period, Bill Wallace, a perceptive sports reporter for the New York *World-Telegram,* the *Herald Tribune* and *The New York Times* (in that order), was also around to see the metamorphosis in Frank Gifford as an athlete and as a person, and to write about it. That made him the logical man to recall Frank Gifford's finest year in sports.

In this, the first of a series of books on the greatest years of the greatest athletes in our sports heritage, the chronicle of Frank Gifford in his big year gives credence to the good that can come out of athletic achievement.

—Murray Olderman

FRANK GIFFORD

THE GOLDEN YEAR 1956

CHAPTER ONE

The 21 Club on New York's West Fifty-second Street is not a club at all but a public restaurant that successfully manages to keep away the poor and the infamous. The establishment itself is famous. Many affairs of state and love have been decided there.

A stern young man just inside the beautiful iron and glass doors greets or turns away those who enter on the basis of their appearance or name. "Good day, Senator. We have you right inside next to the bar." Or, "Sorry, we have no tables. Our reservations are fully booked."

Two large Negro athletes, who never would have put their feet in the place otherwise, formally agreed at 21 to fight one another for New York State's version of the world heavyweight boxing championship. That was early in 1968 and their names were Joe Frazier and Buster Mathis. The announcement of this impending fight was made on the third floor of the 21 Club in the improbably named Hunt Room by representatives of the new Madison Square Garden, where it was to be staged on March 4. Never before had a fight been "announced" in a room decorated with paintings of young women wearing a minimum of clothes fashionable in the 1920's.

The audience in the room was made up largely of working stiffs, meaning members of the press, radio, television and allied communication industries such as public relations and publicity. The workers were to record the fight announcement in their different ways and pass it on to the public, some of whom might buy seats at $100 each to see the action.

One of the workers was Frank Gifford. He was the camera announcer for WCBS-TV, the Columbia Broadcasting System's New York television station. Gifford is the most famous and successful former athlete now in the broadcasting profession. An observer could tell that by watching Gifford during the 95 minutes that he was present.

There was the bedlam that usually accompanies a crowd of media people. There were speeches, by Irving Mitchell Felt, president of the Garden; by Harry Markson, the matchmaker, and by Edwin B. Dooley, the state athletic commissioner. There were questions asked by writers and short answers returned by the fighters.

The significance of those 95 minutes was that, except for the fighters, Frank Gifford, a former professional football player who had last caught a pass in combat way back in 1964, signed more autographs that day than anyone else in the Hunt Room.

The waiters at 21, accustomed to serving dishes like *brandade de morue* (crushed codfish) to people like Jacqueline Kennedy, were edging up to Gifford with a section of menu and a ball point pen. "For my boy, Frank," said one, using the familiarity with which all famous athletes are accosted. "We watch you every night."

Is Frank Gifford, the retired athlete, called upon to sign autographs merely because he is on television five times a week during the WCBS-TV evening news show? No; there is more to it than that.

Howard Cosell, Gifford's competitor from the American Broadcasting Company, has a great deal of television exposure. But under similar circumstances no one asks him for his autograph.

Cosell did not attend the University of Southern California and marry the campus beauty. He was not an all-American football player at U.S.C., nor was he a professional star on five championship teams of the New York Giants. Gifford did and was all of these things before he became a television sports announcer. They all helped.

Gifford's face, once described inaccurately as "devilishly handsome," is before the sports public a great deal. It is a face better known now than when he was a player. "That's because I don't wear a helmet anymore," explains Gifford, a man of mild modesty. "Football players are at a disadvantage when it comes to public recognition. The public can't see their faces behind those face masks."

This is true. Gale Sayers of the Chicago Bears, the best running back in pro football as Gifford once was, spent a recent winter in New York City taking a stock broker's course, and he went unrecognized as he walked about the streets.

But Frank Gifford is recognized, even by the blasé waiters at 21. "I sign more autographs now than when I was a player," Gifford has said.

His fame is attributable to a combination of elements—the memory of his days as a great athlete; his continuing appearances on television as a local New York sportscaster or as a CBS game announcer, as well as the rather pleasant, easy manner that Gifford affects with his television public.

On the occasions when Gifford comes into personal contact with that public, at some sports function for example, the incident that is invariably referred to is the injury caused by Chuck Bednarik. In the fall of 1960 at Yankee Stadium, Gifford was hit on a perfectly executed and legal tackle by Chuck Bednarik, a linebacker for the Philadelphia Eagles and now in the pro football Hall of Fame. Gifford went down—and out of the game—with a concussion.

"I was there," the public is certain to say to him. "If all the people who claim they were there," said Gifford, "actually were there that day, the stadium would have had a quarter of a million people in it. There are even those who insist to me that it happened in Philadelphia, or even Pittsburgh."

It was a dramatic moment, Gifford lying on the frozen turf, Bednarik standing over him with an arm raised in glee because Frank had dropped the football and the Eagles had recovered his fumble.

"A lot of people thought I was dead," said Gifford. "So did I."

There is a demand for autographs from a person who was considered by himself and others to be dead and yet who survived to write his name another day.

It took no special talent to lie on the ground with a concussion. But a lot of skill went into the second most memorable occasion of Gifford's twelve seasons with the New York Giants. In those twelve seasons Gifford caught 367 passes. The most important one and the most impossible one to catch came in the final game of the 1963 season, Gifford's next-to-last campaign.

Many great athletes have passed through the American scene. A very few have left behind those occasions, which served to make their memory an indelible one. There was the afternoon in Chicago when Babe Ruth pointed to the right field wall in Wrigley Field during the 1932 World Series and hit Charley Root's next pitch over that wall. There was the day Hitler walked out on Jesse Owens at the 1936 Olympic games. There was the "long count" in the Dempsey-Tunney fight in 1927.

Gifford's second memorable occasion was The Catch.

The Pittsburgh Steelers were the Giants' opponents in December 1963, at Yankee Stadium. Tie games are not counted in figuring the standings of the National Football League and the Steelers had played three ties that season. Going into the contest against the Giants, Pittsburgh had a 7-3 won-lost record. New York was 10-3.

If the Steelers could win for a final mark of 8-3 their percentage would be .727 and the Giants, with 10-4, would have .714. The Steelers were therefore in a position to win the game and thereby win the eastern conference title.

Few believed they had a chance because New York had a vastly superior team. Buster Ramsey, then a Steelers' assistant coach, told a friend the night before, "We don't belong on the same field with them. But you never know what can happen in a football game."

The Steelers have always been a hard team for the Giants and they were for a while that cold afternoon until Gifford pointed the way.

New York got away smartly for a 16-0 lead. The Steelers gained three points back on a 27-yard field goal by Lou Michaels just before half time. In the third period Ed Brown, the Pittsburgh quarterback and a friend of Gifford's from U.S.C., hit flanker Gary Ballman on a 21-yard touchdown pass. Michaels kicked the conversion and the Steelers were behind by only six points, 16-10.

Could it be that one of the Giants' finest seasons of all time might be wiped out on the last day through an inexplicable loss to an inferior opponent?

After the ensuing kick-off the bald old man for the Giants, Y. A. Tittle, went to work. So far that season Tittle had thrown 35 touchdown passes for an all-time league record. His motto was "Throw the ball." As Kyle Rote once said of him, "If it were not traditional on fourth down to punt, I'm convinced Y.A. would have passed. And with his ability, I would have gone along with him 100 percent."

The New York move began at the 21 yard line. A first-down pass was incomplete. Phil King, the fullback, gained two yards on second down. That brought up a third-down-and-eight situation, which could hardly have been called auspicious.

Tittle had supreme confidence in his third-down calls. Gifford, playing flankerback, was sent down and to the inside, even though Tittle preferred to work against the perimeters of the defenses. Y.A.'s pass was too deep. It should never have been caught.

Somehow Gifford got the fingertips of his right hand on the football and the ball implausibly stuck there.

"All I was trying to do," said Gifford, "was bat the ball up in the air. I didn't think it would stick in my hand."

By the time the Steeler secondary trapped Gifford and dropped him, he was down on their 47-yard line. The play went in the books as a mere 30-yard pass but it proved to be far more than that.

The great catch, the great effort, put fire in the Giants and dismay in the collective Steeler outlook.

Tittle went right back to Gifford on the next play, a pass that Frank took down to the Pittsburgh 22. The next play? Another pass of course: Tittle to Joe Morrison for 22 yards and a touchdown. The Giants went on to win handily, 33-17.

Buddy Parker, the Pittsburgh coach, later said of Gifford's first catch, "That catch did it. If he hadn't caught that ball, who knows?"

It was one more big play for the athlete who made so many big plays. Not only was it a brilliant physical effort, it came under cicumstances of duress and turned a threatened defeat into a magnificent victory.

"Greatest catch I ever saw, Frank."

"Thank you."

"I was there. I seen it. Conerly to Gifford, right?"

"Thank you."

Although the passer was not Charley Conerly, who had retired two years earlier, Gifford has the good sense never to correct his erring public.

The public is inclined to remember and revere athletes who, in a big showdown game, catch by their fingernails a football that cannot be caught.

But Gifford was not always so sought after. When he first came to New York in 1952, pro football did not amount to so very much and those who played it remained strangers to the city.

About 1956 a man walked into an automobile dealer's showroom on Broadway, introduced himself as Frank Gifford and attempted to buy a car. His fraud was exposed. Gifford himself thought it was remarkable that he had attained such notoriety that an automobile salesman was able to discern his imposter. "I was delighted. I had finally arrived in New York," he said.

"In those days," said Gifford in reference to the early and middle 1950's, "no one knew who you were —or cared. We ate at Jake's delicatessen—ham on rye. The modern Giants nowadays are being taken to lunch at places like 21 or The Four Seasons.

"That goes for jobs too—off-season jobs, endorsements, that kind of thing. In the old days you didn't get much. Nobody wanted to hire you for six months. Now they come running at pro football players and stuff money in their pockets."

During Gifford's time pro football changed right in front of his eyes from just another game into the most popular and widely discussed spectator sport in the United States.

It grew wings and flew in the decade of the 1950's. The attendance for National Football League games in 1950 was 1,977,556, or an average game crowd of 25,353. By 1960 the total was 3,128,296 and the game average 40,106. The public's passion for pro football developed city by city. Winning teams brought out the adulation.

This boom began in Los Angeles. While Gifford was in college at Southern California the Rams took three straight western division titles in the National League, 1949, 1950 and 1951.

The Rams had the stars, quarterback Bob Waterfield and end Tom Fears being the most notable, and soon they had the crowds. In 1950 the Rams drew their first home crowd at the Coliseum in excess of 90,000 and that was a record for pro football.

In the first half of the decade, the powerhouse team in the east was the Cleveland Browns. This team had originally belonged to the rival All-America Conference which had been formed at the conclusion of World War II and lasted four seasons. Then the A.A.C. folded and its more successful franchises at Cleveland and San Francisco joined the National League.

The Browns won the championship every season in the A.A.C. and then they won the eastern title for six straight years, 1950-55, in the N.F.L. Cleveland adored the Browns.

In the western division of the National League the balance of power shifted briefly from Los Angeles to Detroit and then on to Baltimore in the late 1950's. Each league city eventually became full of football addicts who filled the stadiums and, for the most part, kept them filled.

The nation's largest city, New York, had been somewhat indifferent although it had had a pro team, the Giants, since 1925. New York's turn to embrace the Giants as they had never been hugged before came in 1956. Gifford, who played the hero role, helped to seal the embrace.

CHAPTER TWO

In 1956 the New York Giants won the National Football League championship, the "World Championship" as it was called. And Frank Gifford won the Jim Thorpe Trophy as the league's outstanding player.

At the beginning of that season these two events seemed possible but hardly probable. Although the Giants had lost only one of their last seven games in 1955, they still wound up in third place in the N.F.L. eastern division, three games behind the Browns. The Cleveland team had dominated the East for so long—six seasons—that few prognosticators were ready to believe that a decline was at hand. The Browns had lost their star quarterback, Otto Graham, through retirement, but they had so many talented players that it seemed that the Cleveland dynasty would continue.

Because they had finished second, only a game and a

half behind Cleveland in 1955, the Washington Redskins were considered a threat, as were the Chicago Cardinals, a team built around the great offensive back, Ollie Matson.

As it turned out, the Browns did miss Graham terribly. It was the Giants, not the Redskins or the Cardinals, who grasped the opportunity presented by the demise of the Browns. The New York team matured into excellence at most of its positions and laid the foundation for a dynasty of its own. Gifford was an important part of the foundation.

The previous season had been a good but not gaudy one for Frank. He had gained 351 yards rushing which put him far behind the league leader, Alan Ameche of Baltimore who had 961, and he caught 33 passes for 437 yards. He was respected as a good all-around back most notable for his versatility rather than for any one skill. Playing at left halfback, he could run, catch, block and throw option passes. He was a star but not one of the magnitude of past Giant heroes like Eddie Price, Bill Paschal, Ward Cuff, Tuffy Leemans or Ed Danowski.

It was in 1925 that the Giants came into the National Football League, which had been founded five years before as a midwest regional organization. Timothy J. Mara, the Giants' founder, paid $500 to establish the franchise which 43 years later had an estimated value of $15 million.

Mara was a bookmaker, an honorable profession in the years before 1939, when pari-mutuel betting was introduced to the New York race tracks. The Maras also had an interest in a coal company and T.J.'s eldest son, Jack, had a small law practice. It was just as well that the Maras, a close-knit family of Irish Catholic origin, had these interests because the football team was in no position to enrich the family or even support it for many, many years.

In the 1920's and early 1930's the team operation was marginal and it improved only slightly thereafter. Even though the Giants were by far the strongest franchise in the East with nine league or division titles in their first 21 years, the club skimped in many ways.

Emlen Tunnell, a star defensive back who later became a coach, broke in as a rookie in 1948. "In my early years with the Giants," he said, "we didn't necessarily get new game jerseys every season. If you wore out your shoes you took them to the shoemaker to be fixed. The equipment man repaired shoulder pads and helmets when he could. It was not like today when they throw away worn equipment and give out new."

The Giants' home attendance made no appreciable upward progress until 1956. The club was averaging less than 30,000 a game while costs and salaries continued to rise. The war with the All-America Conference between 1946 and 1949 had been costly to the Maras, who for a while lost their monopoly in owning the only pro team in the nation's largest city. The Giants even trailed the rival New York Yankees of the A.A.C. in attendance during 1947 and 1948.

The season of 1953 was a disaster for the Giants. The team won only three games, the fewest in its history, and the Maras felt they had to replace Steve Owen, their coach for 23 years.

Owen, a tobacco chewer of the old school, ran a

virtual one-man operation and did little delegating. Pro football, however, had evolved into a highly specialized game played by two platoons of athletes, one for offense and one for defense. Film study and scouting opponents had become far more intensive; offenses had become more complex, and defensive strategy more involved. The modern coach had to be an organization man, like Paul Brown of the Browns, who was held in awe by almost everyone in the game.

Owen's successor was Jim Lee Howell, a former Giant player and assistant coach. Howell, who liked to delegate responsibility, carefully chose a new staff that included two key men. One was Tom Landry, a soft-spoken Texan who continued to play in the defensive backfield through the 1955 season. If Landry did not actually invent the 4-3 defense, which did so much to change the game in the late 1950's, he certainly brought it to new levels of efficiency.

The second key man was Vince Lombardi, a native New Yorker who had been a Fordham classmate (class of 1937) of Wellington Mara, T. J. Mara's younger son. Lombardi was coaching the offensive backs at the United States Military Academy at West Point, New York, under Colonel Earl (Red) Blaik when Howell and Well Mara convinced him that his future lay in pro football. They were right.

The new Giant head coach gave the planning of the offense to Lombardi and that of the defense to Landry. Said Howell, exaggerating and punctuating his comment with his booming laugh, "A famous coach told me once that the job of a head coach is to keep order and see that the footballs are pumped up. I try to do both."

Lombardi, in the winter of 1954, reviewed the films of the Giants' games the season before and made an estimate of the personnel. When summer training began, Lombardi took Gifford aside and said simply, "You're my left halfback." That was all.

It was the same kind of statement that Lombardi was to make to Paul Hornung of the Green Bay Packers five years later with the same good effect.

Lombardi's immediate faith in Gifford was important to Frank. In the last two years of the Owen regime he had moved back and forth from running back on offense to defensive back—and in several games he played the full 60 minutes. This two-way effort, all but unknown in the modern speed-up game of pro football, took a lot out of Gifford.

"I finished the 1953 season weighing 178 pounds," Gifford said. That was almost 20 pounds less than his usual weight of 195. "I was getting the hell kicked out of me and there was not even anyone around to see it happening."

Gifford had begun his long career with the Giants the season before. He joined the team late in its summer training period after having played with the College All-Stars against the Los Angeles Rams, the defending N.F.L. champions, in the annual All-Star game at Chicago in mid-August.

Although Gifford had been a widely publicized all-America at college and the Giants' number one draft choice, Owen was unimpressed. To "Stout Steve," as he was fondly called, rookies were not to be trusted and especially all-America rookies.

The training camp was at Gustavus Adolphus College in St. Peter, Minnesota. Before an intrasquad game there, Owen addressed his rookies: "Men, football is a tough game. The ones who hit the hardest and oftenest will be the winners. Anybody who doesn't want to hit doesn't belong in a pro camp. Your all-America clippings don't mean a thing to me. I'm looking for men who like to get down in the dirt and whip the guy across from them."

A few minutes later, Owen asked Gifford, "Son, are you in shape to play?" Gifford did not know if he was or if he was not, but it was not a time to say no. "Sure, Coach." The first time Gifford carried the ball that afternoon he hit into the hole and cut back to the middle as he had learned to do in college. He took only two steps when a crash came. He went down and was in darkness. When he revived a few moments later, Gifford asked Freddy Benners, the rookie quarterback, what had happened. "He hit you," said Benners and pointed to John Cannady, the Giants' 260 pound middle guard.

Gifford, who had never been hit that hard before, suddenly had a sense of what Owen had meant about hitting, getting down in the dirt and whipping the other guy.

The training season was discouraging. The veteran players did not talk much to the rookies and the coaches seemed aloof, preoccupied. Gifford didn't feel that he was making any progress and he was homesick—homesick enough to attempt an impulsive departure from the camp. Allie Sherman, the assistant backfield coach and only seven years older than Gifford, caught him at the exit to the dormitory. "I'm leaving," said Gifford.

"Let's talk about it first," said Sherman. They went into the coach's small room and Gifford sat on the bed. "I don't think I've got a chance here," said the young athlete just turned 22. "I've tried my best. It doesn't seem good enough."

Sherman was stunned. "Not good enough?" he said. "Listen, Coach Owen and I think you are one of the best rookie backs we've had around here in years. You're a cinch to make this team. You're just homesick."

Gifford stayed. With his confidence somewhat restored, he scored two touchdowns and intercepted two passes in an exhibition game against the Steelers. In the final preseason game, against the Rams in New York, he caught a pass from Conerly for a 45-yard touchdown and played well defensively.

The rookie from Southern Cal was to open the season as the team's starting left halfback but only because Kyle Rote's knee was still in bad shape.

Rote, a famous all-America back at Southern Methodist, had come to the Giants the year before. In later years his teammates were to insist that Rote was the best coordinated all-around athlete among them. Unfortunately his great potential as a running back was irretrievably lost in the summer of his rookie year. Rote stepped in a hole on a dry, dusty high school field at Jonesboro, Arkansas, where the Giants were working out prior to a meaningless preseason game in Memphis, Tennessee.

Rote severely damaged his knee and it was never

quite the same again. It is to his credit that Rote played eleven seasons for the Giants, most of them as an end or flankerback.

At the start of Gifford's first campaign, Rote was still recuperating from the knee surgery. Because Rote was not ready, Owen and Sherman had moved Gifford into the left halfback position.

Gifford and Rote had quickly become friends, a friendship that was to stay with them beyond the stadiums and beyond the football years. They had several characteristics in common. Not only were they good athletes, they were young men with good minds. They were sharp. They knew how to embellish their physical talents by being able to outsmart the opponent. They also had interests in life that exceeded football and each had a wry sense of humor.

Although he had only been up in the big time for one year, Rote had learned a lot and he passed it on to Gifford even though they were ostensibly rivals for the same position. "The trouble with most rookies," said Kyle, "is that they do things without knowing why they do them. To be good in this game you've got to understand it as well as play it."

The Giants opened the 1952 season in the Cotton Bowl against the Dallas Texans. Gifford ran back the opening kick-off for 75 yards. That was to be the offensive highlight of his season. He played in 10 of the 12 games, carried the ball only 36 times for 116 yards rushing and caught five passes.

Rote came back and did well at left halfback and so Gifford was used often on defense. He had a notable game defending against Bill Howton of Green Bay, then the league's leading pass receiver. At the end of the season Gifford was named to the East squad for the annual pro bowl game, which was an honor for a rookie.

The Giants had a 7-5 won-lost record in 1952 and finished just one game behind the Browns. But the team's integrity was all but wiped out the next season as virtually the same players managed to lose nine of 12 games, finishing eight games in back of Cleveland in fifth, or next-to-last, place in the N.F.L. eastern division. Furthermore, the Browns beat the Giants in Cleveland, 62-14.

Gifford again played on both offense and defense. He saw more offensive duty but he had only 157 yards rushing in 50 carries at the end.

The following season brought in the new coaches and the new scheme. Gifford was to be purely a running back. No defense. That suited Frank. "The other way, playing both ways, I knew I wouldn't have a very lengthy career," he said.

Lombardi's offense was new to the Giants but not to pro football. Lombardi was deeply influenced by the fundamentalism of Colonel Blaik, who maintained that football was a simple game. The games were won by the team that blocked and tackled the best, that executed the plays the best.

Lombardi put into the Giants' offense two-man blocking at the point of attack. Double teaming on offense was almost as old as the game itself but in the modern, quick-hitting T-formation offenses, old-fashioned power blocking had been finessed out of the game in favor of what came to be called brush blocking by a single man.

Lombardi believed that power blocking could be restored to pro football and the plays would still retain their initial quickness and speed. He was right.

The new offensive coach also insisted that the Giants have in their attack one of football's oldest plays, the end run or power sweep. Gifford was to be the leading ball carrier on the sweep.

Some years later when he was in command of the Packers, Lombardi said, "With the Giants we ran what is now called the Green Bay sweep. It was the same thing then and Gifford was great at it."

The sweep, meaning an end run behind outside blocks by a pulling guard and the leading fullback, depends for its success upon the timing between the blockers and the ball carrier. As he moves laterally the ball carrier takes a little dip in his route so as to enable the pulling guard to get out in front and set up his block on the outside linebacker. The really good backs, like Gifford and Hornung, could bring the linebacker across the line of scrimmage by just the slightest false hint in their body motion. Once the linebacker had committed himself, it was all the easier for the guard to block him out of the play.

Another feature of the play was its option character. If the guard found he had to block his man to the outside, the runner would cut to the inside. Conversely the runner stayed on the outside if the guard could manage his block to the inside. The ball carrier also had to know when to turn up field behind his fullback and "run to daylight," the phrase made famous at Green Bay by Lombardi.

When executed with precision, this sweep became a big play. Gifford, in his brightest years ahead, was to major in The Big Play.

CHAPTER THREE

Frank Gifford first made the big plays during his junior year in high school at Bakersfield, California. Playing on the varsity for the first time, he was a T-formation quarterback and he threw eight touchdown passes from 10 to 43 yards in five games.

Appreciating what he had in the 16-year-old Gifford, Coach Homer Beatty the next season (1947) changed his offense from a T to a single wing and installed his star at tailback. The Bakersfield Drillers won their conference championship and Gifford was a sensation.

In a game against Roosevelt High, Gifford threw two touchdown passes, ran from scrimmage for 58 and 75 yards, made a block that broke open a long run for a teammate, kicked the extra points and got off a 53-yard punt.

Being a success was meaningful. A decade later he said, "I excelled at nothing until I played high school football. This achievement got me out of a rut. I even became sports editor of the newspaper, the Bakersfield *Blue and White*. But I didn't like writing about myself. So I got Chuck Whitney to write the stories about our football games. But I edited them."

Frank Newton Gifford was born on August 16, 1930, in Santa Monica, California. His father, Weldon Gifford, worked as a laborer in the oil fields, drilling the wells. Opening up a well might take 30 days or a year and Weldon and his wife Lola moved where the work was. There were a lot of towns in which the Giffords stopped: Taft, Watsonville, Stockton, Avenal, Colingo, Long Beach and even a place called Wink, Texas. There were three children, Winona, Wayne and Frank, the youngest.

The senior Gifford, a man small in stature, had grown up on a rugged homestead near Maricopa, California, and sports were foreign to him. He was born in 1900 and the oil fields enabled him to provide a comfortable but modest living for his family.

In 1944, when their youngest son was 14, the Giffords settled in Bakersfield, which became and remains a hometown symbol for Frank. It was then a town with a population of 40,000 and no special distinctions, located in the vastness of central California. Agriculture and oil had brought about its growth in the twentieth century.

"My brother was 20 months older than me," said Gifford. "We were both interested in sports and when we moved into a town with new kids I would be competing against the ones his age. That put me two years ahead of my own age."

Although a fearsome competitor on the sandlots, Gifford had a size handicap when it came to organized football in high school. As a 14-year-old freshman he was five feet seven inches tall and weighed "almost" 120 pounds. He was a benchwarmer for the Bakersfield High lightweight team as a freshman, a playing substitute for the lightweights as a sophomore until he broke a hand. But he did make the varsity basketball and track teams in his sophomore year.

As his junior year began, he had grown two inches and gained 15 pounds thanks in part to a weight lifting program he conducted in the family garage. Gifford made the varsity initially as a third-string end.

But the Drillers' quarterback, Myrl Hume, was killed in an automobile accident two weeks before the season began, so Coach Beatty took a chance and called on Gifford to fill in. He found he had a willing, hard working pupil; and with hard work came success.

By the time his senior football season was over, Gifford had gained a certain notoriety. Beatty was anxious that Frank go on to college at Southern California, the coach's alma mater.

Although no one in the Gifford family had ever been to college, it was the natural goal for such a talented athlete as Frank. But he did not have enough high school credits to qualify for U.S.C. Under California's then easy-going collegiate eligibility rules, however, that was no problem.

Beatty recommended that Gifford attend Bakersfield Junior College for a semester to gain the credits and then go on to Southern Cal which had promised a scholarship. Bakersfield Junior College had a good football coach in Jack Frost and his teams, the Renegades, held their own in the competitive California junior college ranks.

Gifford was now at a point in his life where every goal he sought he found he could achieve. Events were breaking in his favor and he would continue to achieve his goals, with few exceptions, throughout his athletic career and beyond. It was not entirely a matter of good fortune. This young man had developed a good physique, and also had the intelligence to exploit his physical advantage and to work at improving his skills.

"Good luck is a lazy man's estimate of a worker's success." This anonymous quotation would apply to Frank Gifford.

The Bakersfield Renegades had a winning season in 1948 and so did Gifford. In a game against Dixie College, which Bakersfield won by the unlikely score of 91-6, Gifford had touchdown runs of 45, 60 and 89 yards. Big plays. In the final game against Santa Monica Junior College, Jeff Cravath, the head coach at Southern Cal, was in attendance. Bakersfield won easily as Gifford returned a kick-off 80 yards for one touchdown; intercepted a pass and returned it 50 yards for a second; threw a pass for a third, and finished with a 40-yard scoring run for a fourth.

More big plays. Cravath was impressed.

Gifford entered Southern California at midterm. When spring practice began he was one of an impressive group of freshmen in a turnout of over 100 candidates. Gifford and several other freshmen were on the scrub team that took on the varsity in an intrasquad game. Frank threw a 40-yard touchdown pass and ran for another score as the scrubs upset the varsity, 29-0. That caused a stir.

In the fall the Trojans' opening game was against Navy. Jay Roundy, the regular safetyman, was hurt in the first period and Gifford took his place. Bobby Zastrow, the Navy quarterback, threw a touchdown pass to Ted Carson right over Gifford. But before the game was over Gifford had intercepted two of Zastrow's passes and kicked six straight points after touchdown for a Coliseum college record as U.S.C. won, 42-20.

He kicked five more conversions against Washington State and the Los Angeles newspapers referred to him as "The Trojan Toe." He was also playing regularly on defense and occasionally as a reserve tailback on offense.

Against California, Gifford was asked by Coach Cravath to attempt a 20-yard field goal with less than two minutes to play. The Trojans rarely tried field goals and Gifford never had. Gifford made his good and U.S.C. led, 9-7, with a big upset in sight.

But Frank Brunk returned the ensuing kick-off 100 yards for a touchdown and so the Golden Bears won and went on to the Rose Bowl.

When Southern Cal lost to Stanford, Gifford was taken from the stadium to the Good Samaritan Hospital with a ruptured appendix. The next Saturday, however, he was in uniform again just to kick and he made good on three points after touchdown as the Trojans beat U.C.L.A., 21-7, in the final game.

This was the stuff of which heroes are made—especially Southern California heroes. Life was easy for Gifford and exciting. He was on a full athletic scholarship with a campus job and he had savings from summertime work in the oil fields for spending money. He was the subject of adulation on the sprawling campus in downtown Los Angeles and he also had a girl.

Maxine Ewart's background was different from Gifford's. She had grown up in Los Angeles—"without a care or worry," as she once said—and was the daughter of prosperous if not wealthy parents.

Apart from being a football star Frank was "different," she found. She admired his ambition, his determination and his way of almost always finding something to laugh about.

She had been homecoming queen in 1949, an honor that brought her the title of "Queen of Troy." In the old-time Hollywood football movies, the gridiron hero married the campus queen, and Frank and Maxine did not change the script. They were married in June of 1951 when Gifford had one more season to go as a Trojan hero.

His second season, in 1950, had gone against the script. Southern Cal was favored to win the Pacific Coast Conference title and to go on to the Rose Bowl. Instead the team floundered, winning one game, losing six and tying two. The coach, Cravath, was dismissed.

Gifford did have two notable games. He rallied his team from a 20-0 deficit against Washington State to a 20-20 tie. Playing tailback, he directed a 75-yard drive which he began with two pass completions. He then raced off right tackle all the way to the State 25 and followed with a jump pass to Jim Sears that carried to the 10. With time left for one play, Gifford ran the ball over the goal line, and then kicked the conversion to earn the tie.

The Trojans upset powerful Notre Dame, 9-7, in the final game. Gifford was not expected to play because he had a badly injured right leg and could not run.

Near the end of the game, U.S.C. managed to hold off a Notre Dame drive down near its goal line. The Trojans needed a strong punt up field with a minute left to play. Cravath, who regarded Gifford as the finest college clutch player he had known, asked Frank to make the punt, sore leg notwithstanding.

Gifford went on the field and kicked the ball 73 yards over the head of the Notre Dame safetyman.

By this time Gifford was such a hero, and such a good-looking hero, it seemed only natural that Hollywood should call. It did. In the summer of 1951, following his marriage, Gifford had a bit part in a forgettable football film called *That's My Boy*. He was an extra in the football scenes and he performed as a double for Jerry Lewis, kicking the game-winning field goal. In later years Gifford was to see more of Hollywood.

His senior year was a good one although Southern California did not make it all the way to the Rose Bowl. Under Jess Hill, the new coach, Gifford was the regular tailback in the single-wing offense and he also played as a defensive back even though the two-platoon system was in vogue then in college football.

The tailback position eventually lost out as the age

of specialization came to football. But Gifford certainly was suited for it while it lasted. He was expected to run, pass and block; the entire offense was dependent upon his skills.

Said Gifford of the position, "It was tough but I loved it. The tailback has the game to win or lose because so much is expected of him. I liked that challenge. I do my best when a lot is expected of me. I loved every second of it."

In his senior season, Gifford's statistics were most impressive. He rushed for 841 yards, completed 32 of 61 pass attempts for 303 yards, caught 11 passes for 178 yards, intercepted eight passes, scored seven touchdowns, kicked 26 extra points and two field goals.

He played offense and defense in two all-star games, North-South and East-West. He also gained all-America status in a year when the country produced such outstanding backs as Dick Kazmaier of Princeton, Ollie Matson of San Francisco, Vic Janowicz of Ohio State, Hugh McElhenny of Washington and Hank Lauricella of Tennessee.

Gifford's most memorable game was an upset win for the Trojans over California, then ranked the number one team in the nation. The Bears led at halftime, 14-0. Gifford returned the second-half kick-off to his own 30 where he was tackled by Les Richter, Cal's 230-pound all-America linebacker.

On the next play Gifford ran wide on an option maneuver which he had made into a lethal weapon. If the defense came up, Gifford passed. If it stayed back, he ran.

This time the pass opportunity was not there, so Gifford ran. Richter closed on him near the sideline. But Gifford faked to the outside and then made a magnificent cut to the inside. Richter missed the tackle and Gifford ran 70 yards for a touchdown. He also kicked the point after touchdown.

Toward the end of the final quarter a dazzling run by Gifford put the Trojans on the Cal 20. Gifford tried the pass-run option play again. Richter had a good angle and charged Gifford with his arms out, ready to throw Frank out of bounds. So Gifford threw his pass underhanded, like a softball pitcher, the football passing beneath Richter's upraised arms. The ball went straight to Dean Schneider for a U.S.C. touchdown.

With time running out, Gifford raced 48 yards on fourth down to the California 2 where he was caught. Never an outright sprinter, Gifford has said of himself, "For the first 10 yards I could move as fast as anyone. But after 10 yards there were a lot who could catch me."

With time remaining for one play, Gifford threw his weary frame at the California line once more. His 185 pounds went over the goal line to win the game. His teammates carried him off the field on their shoulders.

Coach Hill called the pass to Schneider, "One of the greatest individual plays I've ever seen." There was nothing so surprising about that compliment because Gifford had become the master of The Big Play.

When the National Football League's draft came in January, the Rams had the bonus selection, meaning the chance to make the first selection of all the eligible collegians. There was a wonderful crop that year. The

Rams chose Billy Wade, the quarterback from Vanderbilt. The Giants were the next-to-last team of the 12 to make their first-round selection and they were delighted to find Gifford still available.

Those were the days before the big bonus contracts. The only competition the N.F.L. faced for the new college talent was the Canadian League, which had had minor success in luring Americans north. The Edmonton Eskimos made a pitch for Gifford. The offer was a $6,000 bonus and a $12,000 salary for one season, almost twice as much as the Giants were willing to pay.

Gifford spurned the offer. "It was good money," he said later. "But it would have been a different game up there. I could hardly wait to get into the N.F.L. I wanted to learn some more about the game. By then I'd had enough football to know that there is no limit to what you can learn. It was just that I wanted new professors."

CHAPTER FOUR

Late in the 1955 season, the New York Giants stirred. In the last six weeks of the season the team beat Washington, the Chicago Cardinals, Philadelphia, Baltimore and Detroit and tied Cleveland. The shaping of a championship team was underway. No one knew why—or cared. A pride had evolved without anyone directing it or forming it. This was a pride that would carry the Giants on to six division titles in eight seasons before the pride expired.

What is pride?

"Hard to put words to," said Gifford in later years, although he had been one of the proudest of all.

"We started out as losers back then, 1955. I don't think anyone on the squad, except for Andy Robustelli, had ever played on a championship team.

"Jim Lee Howell made us hard-nosed. There was no

doubt about that. All of a sudden we began to beat people and then we began to believe that no one could beat us. I guess that's what goes into making up pride.

"Once we had it, I mean we had it. Those Giant teams were no powerhouses, let's face it. But an attitude seemed to grow. 'No one could beat us,' we said. Sure, we lost games here or there. But when it came down to the big games, we didn't lose many of those—the ones we had to win."

Who were these Giants that had the pride, that believed no one could beat them?

Kyle Rote was the left end and Ken MacAfee the right end on the offensive team of 1956. By that time Rote was 28 years old and he had been at the position for two years. He had developed some magnificent moves and defensive backs considered him one of the most difficult receivers to cover because, as one put it, he was so "sneaky." "He'll get open. Rote is always going to get open somehow."

Rote was of moderate size, 6 feet tall, weighing 205 pounds. MacAfee was larger, 6 feet 2, 215 pounds, and slower. He came from Massachusetts, played college football at Alabama and was in his third pro season.

The Giants were not a passing team. Their style was to control the ball on the ground. They ranked ninth out of 12 in passing but third in rushing for the 1956 season. They used 499 running plays and passed only 275 times. It was not surprising then that Rote caught only 28 passes in 12 games and MacAfee merely 14. The Giants' offense was best tailored to throwing to Gifford, the halfback, when he was either flanked wide in a double or single flanker formation, or coming out of the tight T formation. Gifford caught 51 passes to rank third in the league behind the leader, Billy Wilson of San Francisco who had 60.

The offensive tackles were Roosevelt Brown and Dick Yelvington. Brown, 6 feet 4 and 245 pounds, was the key man on the offensive line, its best player and especially important for Gifford. The two of them cooperated magnificently on a weak side option play in which Brown was Gifford's shield. If the defense came up to Gifford as he took the ball to the outside, he had the option of throwing a pass, usually to Rote. If the defense, meaning in most cases the cornerback and safety, stayed back, then Gifford ran behind Brown's magnificent open-field blocking.

For a big man, Rosey was extremely fast. "He could knock the cornerback down and then go on and get the safety," said Gifford. "We made a lot of yards that way."

In 1956 Brown was playing his fourth pro season at the age of 24. He had been the team's 27th draft choice, an unknown from Morgan State College with an astoundingly able physique. He made the league all-star team year after year and played for the Giants right through 1965 when phlebitis ended his career. He then became an assistant coach for the Giants.

Yelvington was smaller, 6 feet 2, 235 pounds, 27 years of age. He came from Florida and was with the Giants for six seasons, through the 1957 campaign.

Bill Austin, later to become the head coach of the Pittsburgh Steelers, was the left guard. From Oregon, he was on the small side, 6 feet 1, 225 pounds, but had a long tour with the Giants, from 1949 to 1957 with two years, 1951-1952, spent in the service.

The right guard was another who had a lengthy career with the Giants, Jack Stroud. He arrived in 1953, an Ohio boy who had attended the University of Tennessee, and he did not depart until 1964. Stroud, 6 feet 1, 235, overcame the handicap of bad knees and was an effective blocker at guard or tackle. He helped to protect the quarterbacks, Heinrich, Conerly and Tittle, on teams that won six division titles and one league championship.

Stroud had a lot of the they-can't-beat-us pride and so did the center, Ray Wietecha. He too lasted a long time in New York, from 1953 to 1962. "Ten good years," he was later to say, "damn good years."

The interior of an offensive line must work together like the pistons and crankshaft of an automobile engine. There can be no weak link. The five men on the Giants' line had, by 1956, three years of playing as a unit and except for Brown at 24, they were all 27 years of age, which is about the time a pro player reaches his peak. Not especially big, they were very quick, notably Wietecha. In coaching terms they "came off the ball real well," meaning they hit into the defense as a unit on the movement of the ball from Wietecha to his quarterback.

Howell deployed his quarterbacks in a rather odd manner. The starter invariably was Heinrich, who had been an all-America at the University of Washington, and was now playing his third year as a professional. He was 25, seven years younger than Conerly. Although

Heinrich was never a particularly brilliant or accurate passer, he began the games at quarterback on the premise that the team could better probe the defenses before Conerly came on. Charley, a dry, silent Mississippian, usually came into the games at the start of the second quarter and went the rest of the way.

The Giants scored more points with Conerly at the helm than with Heinrich. The arrangement seemed hardly justified but it proved to be successful and Howell stuck with success.

Conerly had been a Marine in the South Pacific during World War II. He had seen death in combat and whatever happened thereafter on a football field failed to move "old Cholly," as he was called.

An example would be the adroit manner in which Conerly threw the ball away when something went wrong. If Conerly saw that the odds of completing a pass were going against him, he would neatly throw the ball out of bounds but never obviously. Opponents screamed that Conerly was being deliberate and therefore deserved a penalty for intentional grounding, but few officials called him on it.

Conerly had begun with the Giants in 1948. He played on a number of losing teams in the early years at the Polo Grounds. The disappointed fans and the press were highly critical of him because they were not very well informed about football and the quarterback is the easiest to single out for criticism.

Conerly seemed stoic about the booing but it did hurt him. He continued to do his job and as the cast around him improved, so did the quarterback. The Lombardi-Howell ball control offense suited him well and he became adroit at deceptive ball-handling. The "belly series," which Lombardi brought from West Point into the pro game, required the quarterback to place the football in the belly area of a running back, hold on to it, take two steps with the runner in what was called a "ride," then remove the ball and give it someone else. The purpose of the ride was to freeze the linebackers, who had to wait to see who would end up with the football.

Another form of deception was play action. This was a simpler way of accomplishing the same goal—to freeze the defense momentarily. Play action meant to indicate a running play was coming up by means of fake handoffs to the running backs. Then the quarterback dropped back to pass. The faking was a big help for the receivers, seeking to break free from their downfield defenders.

Although his passing statistics of necessity were below the league leaders, Conerly had by 1956 become a superior quarterback. Of the league regulars, he was the leader in fewest interceptions—7 out of 174 passing attempts. He was a safe quarterback who made very few mistakes.

In his selection of plays and analysis of defense, Conerly enjoyed help. Rote and Gifford in particular were wise informants who had a unique feel for what play or series of plays would work best to keep the offense moving. Conerly accepted their judgement unfailingly.

Apart from Gifford, the team's running backs were Alex Webster and Mel Triplett. Webster, the right halfback, was new to the team in 1955. He had played college football at North Carolina State although he was a New Jersey boy. The Washington Redskins drafted Webster but cut him because he was said to be "too slow." A lot of people said that about Webster during the ten years he carried the Giants to so many successes. He was big for a halfback of the time, 6 feet 3, 225 pounds, and his strong point was an ability to cut sharply into the right blocking hole at exactly the right time.

Webster came to the Giants from the Canadian League where he had played two seasons for the Montreal Alouettes. He led New York in ground gaining in 1955 with 634 yards to Gifford's 351.

Said Gifford of Webster, "Alex had more power than I did. He got the rough calls when we needed three yards in the clutch. He made my sweeps and reverses go by making the defense close inside the tackles where he was best. It was that simple. I was a better player because he helped to open up the outside."

In the Giants' championship year, Webster gained 694 yards rushing and was seventh in the league standings, two places below Gifford who gained 819. Triplett, the 215-pound fullback, was 14th with 515 yards. This trio was easily the league's most effective rushing backfield.

Triplett, in his second pro season, came from Toledo. He served the team well as a blocker and as a straight-ahead runner with more power than finesse. The draw plays—the drop and fake pass by Conerly with a subsequent handoff to the fullback—were especially effective for Triplett.

This was a well-rounded and balanced offensive unit but hardly an overwhelming one. The team scored

264 points in 12 regular season games, an average of 22, which made it no better than fifth best. It ranked seventh in total yards gained but significantly only two teams ran more plays from scrimmage. The Giant method was to hold on to the ball and the method worked.

As a result the defense benefited because the players on that platoon had some time to rest on the sidelines. The defense in turn handed the ball over to the offense with solid regularity. While the Giants' offense had 849 plays, opponents were able to execute only 790 plays against the defense.

Unlike the New York offense which had some years of ripening together, the defense came up to the 1956 season with several new parts. It was a credit to Landry's teaching that the unit quickly developed cohesiveness and team play. Landry's concept of the way the defense should play—in the 4-3 alignment—was not so intricate. However, it required absolute discipline and if any player did something other than what he was supposed to do—like inadvertently going to the rescue of a teammate—there would be trouble.

This defense had its beginning in 1956 and enjoyed a good but not great season. The great seasons were to come later, most notably in 1958 and 1959 when the defense took the Giants into two championship games against the Baltimore Colts. By then experience had been added to skill.

The 1956 starting defensive unit had four new players and one—Sam Huff at middle linebacker—was a rookie. Other newcomers were Andy Robustelli, right end from the Los Angeles Rams; Dick Modzelewski, left tackle from the Pittsburgh Steelers, and cornerback Ed Hughes also from the Rams. Two of the front four then—Robustelli and Modzelewski—were new Giants, the others being Walt Yowarsky at left end and the huge Roosevelt Grier at right tackle. Rosey, 6 feet 5 and 290 pounds in his second pro season, was the biggest man in the league. Yowarsky, a veteran, had joined New York in 1955.

The outside linebackers were Bill Svoboda who had been around since 1954 and Harland (Swede) Svare, acquired from the Rams in 1955. Dick Nolan, in his third New York season, was the other cornerback with little Jimmy Patton, a rookie in 1955, and Emlen Tunnell, in his ninth pro season, at safety. Tunnell, Svoboda and Robustelli were the old-timers on a unit that averaged just 25 years of age.

The Giant defenders gave up 197 points or 16.4 per game for the fourth lowest average in the league. Landry had the emphasis in the right place as New York's defense yielded fewer yards than any other in the league.

Young Huff was a key operator. The 4-3 defense was designed so that the middle linebacker stood the best chance of bypassing the offensive blocking. The man in the middle was supposed to make the largest percentage of the tackles against the run and to make them all over the field. A tackle in college, Huff adjusted well to the unfamiliar middle linebacking position. Although he weighed 230 pounds the West Virginian had plenty of speed for pursuit and he loved to hit. Many of his stinging tackles brought the ball carrier down way over on the sidelines.

Huff became the subject of intense fan adulation. The fans were not sophisticated enough to understand that Sam was making the tackles by design rather than entirely on his own. The praise that came Huff's way seemed excessive but the Giants did not care as long as the team continued to win.

Huff almost left the Giants in their championship season. Like Gifford a few years before, this rookie had become discouraged with his apparent lack of progress in the training camp. Huff found another scared, discouraged rookie in Don Chandler, later to become a brilliant kicking specialist. They decided to leave together. Huff's departure was interrupted by Ed Kolman, the line coach, who told Sam he was being foolish; he had more talent than the other rookies and he just needed time to learn what was expected of him. Sam agreed to stay but decided to accompany his buddy, Chandler, to the airport. The plane was one hour late. Homesick for his mountain town of Farmington, Huff wavered in his resolve to stay.

A car drove up and out jumped Lombardi. "Hold on," he said. "You may not make this ball club, Chandler, but you're sure as hell not quitting on me. And neither are you, Huff, in case you've got any ideas about running out." The two players meekly got in Lombardi's car and went back to the training camp.

Said Huff later, "If that plane had been on time, Chandler would have been on it. And maybe I would have too."

When the season opened a few weeks later and the great adventure that was to lead to a championship began, both were full-fledged members of the Giants.

This one is about to be caught—and then off and away for a TD. Lonnie Sanders of the Redskins is defending. *Daniel R. Rubin*

Will He Run or

Against the Redskins in 1960, he throws to Bob Schnelker—not seen in the pictures.

Daniel R. Rubin

Will He Pass?

But, against the Browns in 1959, he kept the ball and went for a touchdown. *Daniel R. Rubin*

Just before throwing to Alex Webster.

Daniel R. Rubin

George Shaw has handed off and Giff is now moving against the Eagles. *Daniel R. Rubin*

Frank makes a back-handed catch against the Steelers. *Daniel R. Rubin*

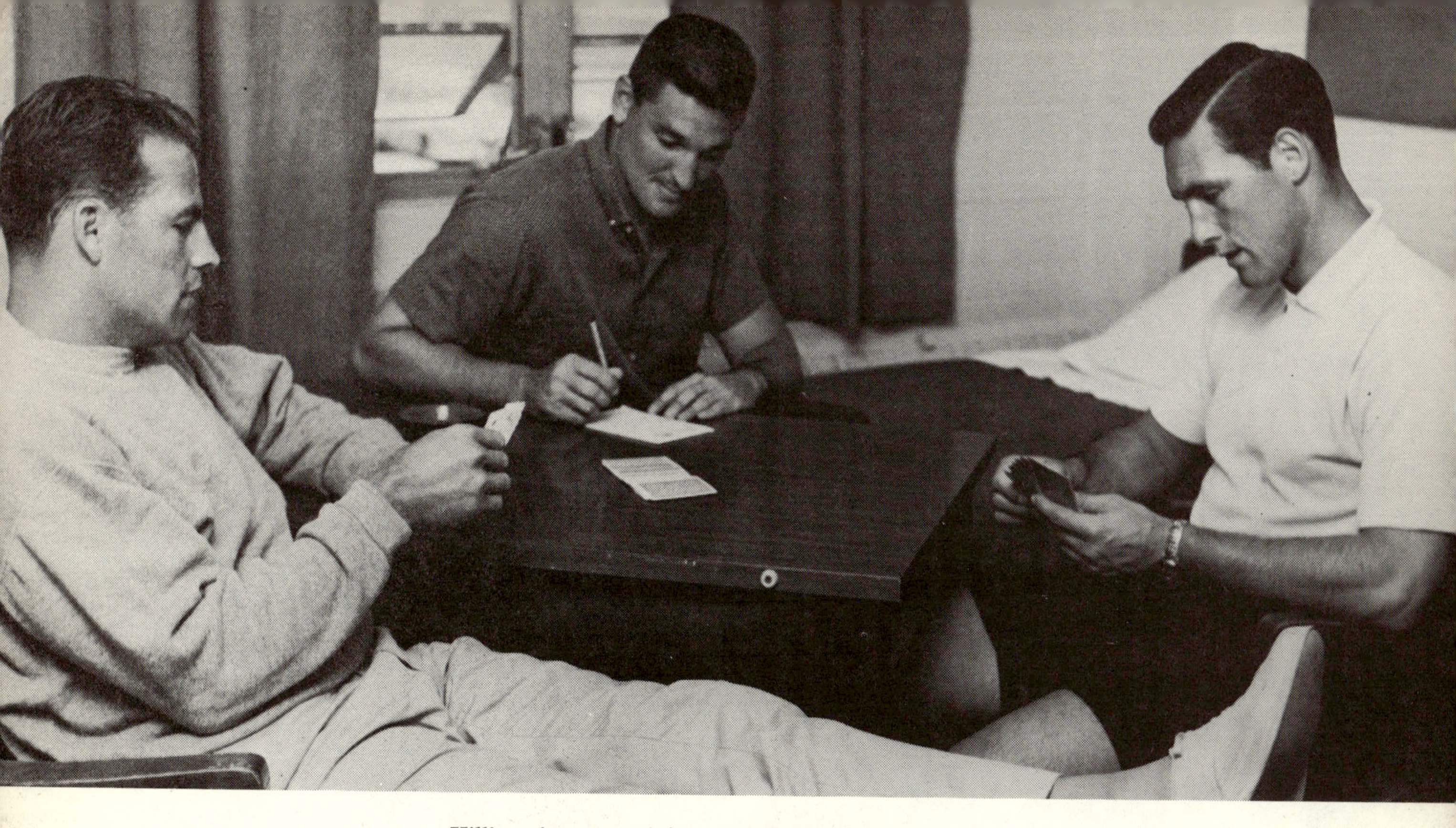

Killing time at training camp with Phil King and Ralph Guglielmi. *Daniel R. Rubin*

To the victors—come the press.
Daniel R. Rubin

Gifford as a student at the University of Southern California.
University of Southern California

With Tittle on the sideline during the last game for both of them.

CHAPTER FIVE

Frank Gifford's golden year began on September 30, 1956 against the 49ers in Kezar Stadium, San Francisco, which is about as far from Bakersfield going north-northwest as is Los Angeles going south-southwest.

It was an auspicious beginning. The Giants won the game, 38-21 and victory came easily. New York opened up a 24-0 lead before the first half was over and then coasted. It was the first time the 49ers had ever lost a home opener.

Gifford booted a 17-yard field goal for New York in the first period. The field goal proved significant as it was the second and last one he would ever kick successfully for the Giants (the other had come in 1953). Frank also added four conversion kicks following four touchdowns as he was for the moment the team's place-kicker.

Ben Agajanian, a ubiquitous kicker lacking the big toe on his right and therefore key foot, was then negotiating his contract with management. Aggie, who had been knocking about pro football since 1945, wanted to be a commuter kicker. His idea was to fly in for the Sunday games from his home in Long Beach, California. Well Mara would have none of it.

It is rather ironic that eight years later the Giants traded Don Chandler, an outstanding kicker, to Green Bay, ostensibly because Chandler too wanted to be a commuter kicker. It was against team policy, said Mara. Nevertheless, the Giants wound up with a commuter kicker, Pete Gogolak, in the 1967 season and were glad to have him. Gogolak was in the Army at Fort Belvoir, Virginia, and reported to the Giants the day before each game. No one mentioned policy.

In the absence of Agajanian, who had been the Giants' leading scorer the previous two seasons, the club turned to Gifford. Although Frank had been a fine kicker in college, he had done very little kicking in the pro ranks and lacked Agajanian's distance.

The San Francisco game was one of big plays for the Giants, a team that had little reason to be described as explosive.

Don Heinrich, the starting quarterback, threw a 44-yard pass to Webster for the first touchdown. Gifford ran 59 yards for the second. Heinrich then threw a scoring pass to Triplett—a 35-yard play that brought the score to 24-0.

The touchdown pass to Triplett was unusual, the

only scoring one he caught all season. He had what were called "iron hands" because he dropped the ball so often. "We'd throw to Mel occasionally just to keep the defenses honest," said Howell. "They seldom bothered to cover him." In the 1956 season Triplett caught only five other passes for a total gain of just 13 yards. No one kept figures on how many he dropped.

Ray Beck, who started at middle linebacker because the discovery of Huff was not yet complete, later intercepted a pass by Y. A. Tittle, then the San Francisco quarterback, and that led to another touchdown by Triplett, from the one. Dick Nolan, the left cornerback, also intercepted a Tittle pass and returned it eight yards to the San Francisco 22 in the fourth quarter. Triplett scored two plays later from the 13.

Hugh McElhenny, a longtime friend and competitor of Gifford's, scored two touchdowns for the 49ers, who were unsuccessfully playing catch-up football.

What did Gifford a dozen years later remember of the game?

"My run. What else?" said he. It was a typical Gifford comment, one of facetious braggadocio. But he certainly had retained the details of the run.

"The play was '47 power' run off the belly series. The quarterback's ride was to the fullback and then the handoff was to me. One guard pulled and took the linebacker. I cut and found there was nobody there so I went for a ride downfield. I was sprinting. If I'd had to run any further I don't think I would have made it."

Lombardi and Ed Kolman, the offensive line coach, had worked out "47 power" late the season before. The idea was to get some two-man power blocking in the off-tackle running holes. In the Giants' numbering system the holes are designated as seven on the right side, six on the left side. Gifford, the left halfback, was the No. 4 back and Webster, the right halfback, the No. 2 back. So "47" was Gifford through the No. 7 hole running from left to right and "26" was Webster running the play to the other side, right to left.

Lombardi and Kolman reasoned that there was so much man-on-man brush blocking in the pro T formation offenses that an old fashioned double-team block might take some defenses by surprise. "There's not a lineman in the game who can handle a double-team block," said Lombardi.

In "47 power," the offensive right end, MacAfee, and right tackle, Yelvington, double-teamed the defensive left end. Bill Austin, the left guard who had pulled out, took the left linebacker to the outside with help if needed from fullback Triplett, the lead blocker. So there were two double-team blocks and between them a hole for Gifford.

It was the kind of play that the Giants needed to make any progress. Howell reflected years later, "We didn't have much outright power up front. Take Wietecha. He was awfully quick and therefore awfully good. Stroud? He was strong. Yelvington? He wasn't strong. He knew his limitations. He'd tell me over and over, 'Coach, nobody's going to eat me up.'

"He was about right. Nobody did eat him up so you could count on a standoff there. But to win games you need more than standoffs. When we could get a double-team block on the end, it helped us."

It might be an exaggeration, but only a mild one,

to say that "47 power" brought back to pro football a basic fundamental—the double-team power block—that had been allowed to slip away with the advent of the quick-hitting T formation offenses. All modern pro teams use double-team blocking and run plays similar to "47 power."

The Giants were willing to settle for a four-yard gain with such plays and therefore sustain their ball-control offense. But Gifford made four yards into 59 yards and a touchdown against the 49ers. Why was that?

"It beats me," he said. "Some defensive back must have gotten lost."

Gifford tested his memory some more. "It seems to me," he said, "in that game I caught a key pass for about 50 yards, but not a touchdown. It was a cross-over pattern underneath. That was new stuff in those days. The defenses didn't know how to handle it. I ran that play dozens of times. The Giants must have used it hundreds of times. It always seems to work."

It is not a complex play but the timing has to be just right. Gifford was excellent at making the timing come out just right. He was flanked to the right, outside of the right or tight end, MacAfee. The end ran a down-and-out pattern, Gifford down and to the inside. The two crossed and Gifford wound up "underneath" the defense, meaning somewhere in between the secondary and the line of scrimmage.

It is difficult for defensive backs to cover crossing receivers. The defenders are likely to be distracted, or even confused, just long enough so that the receiver can break into the clear.

This maneuver is not unlike basketball's pick play in

which a defender is screened out of the action. The pick play is allegedly illegal in football but the Giants over the years have run many a successful pick without being called for it. Identification of a pick play is a "judgement call" on the part of the officials and few of them seemed concerned enough to throw down a penalty marker.

There was no more able pick-play combine in pro football than Rote and Gifford, those champions of chicanery.

Anything further about that 49ers game? "It sure got me off to a good start," said Gifford. "I think it was after that game that some writer—I forget who it was—said now that I was doing the kicking I had a chance to finish among the first ten players in rushing, receiving and scoring for one season. No one had ever done that before. The idea intrigued me."

Football statistics to most coaches are meaningless. "Except for the final score," says Allie Sherman, "statistics are for losers." Or for 12-year-old fans. Why was Gifford intrigued?

"Everyone has pride in his achievements," he replied. "If you accomplish something unique, it has meaning. Sure, somebody else is going to come along eventually and do better—records are made to be broken. Still, it's nice. Besides, it comes in handy when talking contract. You can make more money the next year."

That was Frank Gifford talking, a man of pride and practicality.

Although he stopped kicking, Gifford did reach this

achievement. At the end of the season he ranked fifth in rushing yardage, third in number of passes caught and tenth in points scored.

The kicking experience was soon to end. The following Sunday Gifford missed a conversion placement as the Giants lost to the Chicago Cardinals in Chicago, 35-27.

In the third game Gifford kicked two conversions in a 21-9 victory over Cleveland but Don Chandler handled the third one. Frank also missed a field goal attempt, the last he ever tried for New York. Said Gifford, "I think I kicked the ball right into Wietecha's rear end. Carlton Massey of the Browns picked the ball up and lateraled to Galen Fiss—he ran about 50 yards with it before I tackled him."

By the Sunday of the next game Agajanian had resolved his problems with management and rejoined the team—as a noncommuter. Gifford was not sorry. "As a kicker," he said, "I couldn't concentrate enough. There was too much else for me to do out on that field, to have to think about. I couldn't have done it. Besides, my legs would have gotten too tired."

In the next game, against the Cardinals, the Giants' defense came apart completely and that was to happen only one other time all season. Before a modest crowd of 21,798 at Comiskey Park, a quarterback of no special distinction named Lamar McHan was a star. He scored two touchdowns against New York and passed for two more.

The Giants started out right. They recovered a fumble by Matson at the Chicago 25 and Mel Triplett scored from the two-yard line four plays later. The point after touchdown was the one that Gifford missed.

The Cardinals led at the half, 14-13, and went out in front in the third quarter.

Gifford has no memory of this game, except for Matson. "I always liked to watch him," said Frank. "He was such a great ball carrier. I'm glad I didn't have to play defense against him."

Oliver G. Matson was an all-America at the University of San Francisco. He and Gifford came into the league in the same year, 1952. They were never exactly rivals and poor Matson, who played for 14 seasons or two more than Gifford, was seldom a member of a winning team and never a championship one.

Both Gifford and Matson were voted to the eastern division all-star teams in the middle 1950's before the Cardinals traded Ollie to the Rams for seven players in 1959.

Howell was once asked by a newspaperman if he would consider trading Gifford for Matson. Jim Lee, who had often been an outspoken critic of Gifford's, bridled. Said he, "I'm not knocking Matson whom I would like to have. But certainly not for Gifford. Matson is faster and runs harder, but Frank is a superior passer and receiver. Nor is there anything wrong with my man's running. Gifford is like a coach on the field. He sizes up situations and reacts quickly. My vote goes to Gifford over Matson."

It is common for a player like Gifford to admire and study a counterpart such as Matson. "It's not that you try to pick up things," Gifford explained. "Everybody has their own style. I suppose you watch the other guy to see how he does it as much out of curiosity as anything else. There are a lot of reasons." Inspiration is one.

Gifford's teammate, fullback Mel Triplett, was always at his best when the Giants were playing a team that had a good fullback. "That seemed to inspire Mel," said Howell. "He wanted to show up the other fellow, to prove to the people he was the best. Some of Triplett's best games for us were against the Browns when they had Jimmy Brown."

Brown was playing for Syracuse University in 1956 and did not reach the Browns until the next season. His predecessor at fullback for Cleveland was Ed Modzelewski, called Big Mo. His younger brother Dick played defensive tackle for the Giants and was called Little Mo. He was one inch shorter but 50 pounds heavier.

When the Giants came into Cleveland on October 14 the Browns were in trouble for the first time since coach Paul Brown had put together his first Cleveland team a decade before. The Browns had been an undistinguished football team in losing to the Cardinals, 9-7, and beating Pittsburgh 14-10, the week before.

Cleveland had no scoring punch, although the defense still seemed solid. George Ratterman, long an understudy, had succeeded Otto Graham at quarterback. Up to this season the Browns had had only one quarterback, Graham, and he put them in a championship game every year.

Ratterman was not to be the answer and that became plainly evident in the 21-9 loss to the Giants. Later in the season the Browns shifted to Tommy O'Connell but they had the first losing campaign in their history with a 5-7 won-lost record and averaged only 13.9 points a game.

Although relatively new, the Giants-Browns rivalry had become as intense as any in the N.F.L. because of the many great games the two teams had played. After six seasons the series standing was nine victories for Cleveland, five for New York and one tie. The Giants had not beaten the Browns since 1952 but they had tied them the year before, 35-35.

The 1956 game in Cleveland attracted a crowd of 60,042 to the municipal stadium, the largest attendance there in three years. The crowd was a sullen one and largely silent as the Giants completely dominated the Browns both on offense and defense.

The defense held Modzelewski and halfback Fred Morrison to 40 yards rushing and the harassed Ratterman lost 62 yards in the second half while attempting to pass. The only Cleveland touchdown came after Gifford's field goal was blocked.

The other two points were a worthless gift from Charley Conerly right at the end of the game. The Giants put up a goal line stand. On fourth down Big Mo was stopped by his brother, Little Mo, one foot away from a touchdown. The Giants took over and Conerly ran three quarterback sneaks to the one yard line. On last down he ran this way and that in the end zone, helping to kill the clock, and he finally downed the ball, giving Cleveland a safety.

The Giants made three long drives and Webster scored at the end of each one. Alex, Gifford and Triplett pounded away at the Cleveland defense as the Giants' ground attack controlled the ball and the game. Gifford was the leading gainer with 73 yards. Conerly threw just enough passes to maintain an honest Cleveland defense.

A key one was to Gifford coming out of the backfield on a fake running play from the Browns' 19. Frank carried the short pass down to the Cleveland one and Webster scored from there.

A quarter of the season had by then gone by and the Giants found themselves in second place in the eastern division, tied with Philadelphia which had also won two of its three games. The Cardinals were unbeaten and, most significantly, Cleveland's old champions were two full games out of first place after only three had been played.

"We felt we had a pretty good ball club," said Howell. "But there was still a long way to go."

CHAPTER SIX

Jack Mara, the longtime president of the New York Giants who died in 1965, enjoyed humor as much as any man. One time he was complimented about a new Lincoln Continental he had just acquired. "I have three luxuries," he replied. "My wife, my automobile and my taxi squad."

Mara enjoyed telling the following story—apocryphal or not, no one will ever know. In the winter of 1957 after the Giants had won the National Football League's "world championship," Mara was discussing a new contract with one of the offensive linemen. The man sought a raise that Mara felt was too large.

The athlete had stated his case and the owner remained unimpressed. So the player blurted out this reasoning: "Without my blocking Gifford never would have had a great year."

Mara's bushy eyebrows lifted. "How do you know that?" he asked.

"Because," said the player, "Gifford told me so all season."

Football is and always will be a game in which the blockers do the heavy work while those who throw, catch and run with the football gain all the credit. Gifford constantly attempted to redress the inequity as best he could. "I've always complimented them, thanked them for what they did for me," he said of his blockers. "I'd do anything to keep them happy. I knew I couldn't do without them, although the public never seemed to realize it."

Within the family of the Giants' players, Gifford was more of a pacesetter than a leader. He came from a big-city college and had acquired a sophistication that few sons of California oil well riggers could hope to achieve. The less urbane players, especially the younger ones, looked up to Gifford. For them he set the example, but more in the area of what kind of sports jacket to buy rather than the best way to make a cross body block.

In the early years Gifford was very much within the family of players. Later he began to slip away as he made more money and became more famous although those were not the reasons for the slippage. At heart Gifford was always somewhat of a loner. Fame brought him into an orbit of interests and people apart from football and football players. These exposures interested him and he turned to them.

When Gifford returned to the Giants after a one-year retirement, his two best friends, Rote and Conerly, were no longer there. He became more distant than ever from the family of players—to the point where he was almost aloof. Still he was admired, if from afar.

One evening at training camp in Fairfield, Gifford was seen driving away from the dormitory in his wife's new white Mustang convertible. "That Frank, he sure is class," said one younger player to another. "All class and he gets away with it. How much money do you suppose he's making? Hundred thousand a year?"

"I wouldn't doubt it," said the other and spat. "Nice guy too."

Gifford was stuffing his blockers with compliments in October and November of 1956 when the Giants took off on a five-game winning streak which lifted them into a tie for first place in the standings.

After the victory over the Browns in Cleveland, they beat Pittsburgh, Philadelphia, the Steelers again and then the Cardinals.

The first Pittsburgh game was played in the Giants' new home, Yankee Stadium, on October 21. The attendance came to 48,108, the largest crowd the team had ever had for a home opener. That day marked the beginning of an era of unprecedented prosperity for the franchise.

The Giants had always played at the Polo Grounds, the home of the baseball Giants. But the Polo Grounds had come upon hard times. There was next to no parking adjacent to the old stadium and the neighborhood at the north end of Seventh Avenue had long been deteriorating.

The Maras had made a deal with Dan Topping, president of the Yankees, to move their operation across the Harlem River to Yankee Stadium. There was more parking available, the surroundings were more attractive and the stadium was somewhat larger, although no one then envisioned the endless series of capacity crowds that were to develop in the 1960's.

Horace Stoneham, the football Giants' longtime landlord, did not seem to mind the departure of the tenant and the resulting loss of revenue. Although no one knew it at the time, Stoneham was even then contemplating moving his baseball operation elsewhere, to Minneapolis or to San Francisco. He elected to go to California with Walter O'Malley and the Dodgers, both teams abandoning New York after the 1957 baseball season.

The Maras' Giants flourished immediately in "The House That Babe Ruth Built." That first crowd was the largest that the team had attracted since 52,880 saw the Giants beat the 49ers back in 1952. Six games at the Polo Grounds had drawn 163,787 in 1955. Six dates at the Stadium the next year, admittedly with a winning team on display, drew 280,727.

Giants' home attendance continued to soar until 1962 when saturation was reached, all seven games selling out for a total of 441,000.

The athletes liked the Stadium because their locker room was far more luxurious than the cramped cell block at the Polo Grounds. But they came to be suspicious of the playing field. It was not quite level, they said. If you were moving toward center field, toward the open end of the stadium, you were going uphill.

Psychologically the offensive players preferred to operate in a downhill direction.

In later years it was established that the players' suspicions were substantially correct—by a matter of a few inches.

To Gifford's pixilated sense of humor the concept of and up and down football field was divine. In the championship game against the Chicago Bears at the end of the season he caught a pass from Conerly and ran uphill. It was a 67-yard play, and although it did not score a touchdown, it was the longest play of the season for the Giants. Stan Wallace, the Bears' defensive back, caught Gifford from behind and tackled him on the Chicago nine.

"If I'd been running downhill rather than up, he never would have caught me," said Gifford.

The Giants' first game in the Stadium was a good one for them. They scored 38 points to 10 for the Steelers, gaining 455 yards on offense to 168 for Pittsburgh.

The home team started off slowly and Conerly came in at quarterback a little earlier than usual, in this case late in the first quarter. He was hot that afternoon, completing 14 of 23 pass attempts for 208 yards, and three touchdowns.

On the Giants' initial scoring drive—80 yards in 13 plays—Conerly completed five of eight passes, the last one from the 14 to MacAfee in the end zone.

Ted Marchibroda, the Pittsburgh quarterback, fumbled and Svoboda recovered for New York at the Steeler 29 to open the second scoring shot. Conerly passed to Gifford for eight yards to the 21 and then to Webster for the touchdown.

Lombardi, sharp at picking up weaknesses, had found one in the Pittsburgh secondary. Henry Ford, the right halfback was a poor coverer of receivers. So Conerly picked on Ford all afternoon with Gifford and Rote the receivers.

The Giants, a smart team rather than a great team, always searched for the weaknesses, trying to establish an advantage if they could. Gifford, the top receiver, was flanked out to the right or left depending from game to game on the opponent's most vulnerable defensive halfback. In Pittsburgh's case Ford was it and not Jack Butler, an all-pro on the other side.

From the solid T formation with the three backs side by side—Howell called it "the full deck"—Gifford ran for 16 yards on a trap play. Then he took a pass from Conerly for a first down on the 11 and Agajanian kicked a field goal as time ran out in the second period.

In 3½ minutes the Giants had scored 17 points to break open the game. Their halftime lead was 17-3. In the third quarter a Conerly-Gifford pass gained 31 yards to the Pittsburgh 30 and four plays later Gifford scored from the 2 on a standard off-tackle slash.

The Giants' last score was made by Gene Filipski, a speedy halfback who was Gifford's reserve and therefore seldom played. In 12 games he carried the ball only 13 times and this was his big gainer of the season, a 35-yard touchdown run. Filipski had played for Lombardi and Red Blaik at West Point in 1950 but he was dismissed from the Academy in the cribbing scandal of 1951 and finished his college career at Villanova. In 1956 he was a 25-year-old pro rookie.

While with the Giants and later at Green Bay, Lombardi insisted in going with his best. He repeatedly turned aside Howell's suggestions that Gifford on occasion be relieved. Said Vince with regard to Gifford, "He's the one we are going to win with, so let's stay with him."

Against the Steelers that afternoon Gifford caught six passes from Conerly for a total of 104 yards. He dropped none. In that entire season Gifford did not drop more than two or three although coaches often worried that he might because of Frank's strange habit of catching the football "backwards."

A great many pass receivers do their business with one hand, the left, extended slightly above the other. If the ball is thrown high, they will reach for it with the left hand and secure the catch with the right. Gifford did it the other way, the right hand uppermost. It looked rather odd although no coach he ever had was foolish enough to try to get him to "correct" his style.

"I did it backwards," he said. "I don't know why. I just couldn't catch the ball any other way." No, Gifford is not left-handed.

The game against the Steelers was the Giants' fourth. After it was over they took sole possession of second place, one game behind the Cardinals who had won their first four. Cleveland had lost again and was now three games behind the leader, two behind the Giants.

The next Sunday the Giants played the Philadelphia Eagles in Yankee Stadium before a crowd of 40,960 which *The New York Times* saluted as "a banner turnout." The Giants won, 20-3, and tied for first place with a 4-1 won-lost record because the Cardinals were upset by Washington. Cleveland lost again and the Browns now were three games behind the Giants.

Although the Giants won easily, Howell had begun to talk like a winning and therefore worrying coach. He said in appraising the victory, "We were ragged, we fumbled and we didn't pass enough."

The Eagles were reputed to have a good defense, one coached by Steve Owen, the former Giant mentor now an assistant to Hugh Devore. Heinrich started the game at quarterback for New York as usual. Explained Howell, "Teams are coming out with a lot of odd defenses against us. Heinrich is good at sizing up these defenses and calling automatics."

Heinrich moved the Giants twice in the first period within field goal range for Agajanian, who kicked two from the 20 and 39-yard lines.

A favorite and famous Giant play, the weak side pitch, worked for Gifford and Conerly and Rosey Brown in this game.

Webster flanked out to the right, the strong side. Gifford, at left halfback, lined up behind Brown, the left tackle. Rote, the left end, split out a few yards. Usually he served as a decoy on this play, going deep. But the Eagle right linebacker dropped off the line of scrimmage and Rote had to block him to the inside, which he did.

The Giants on previous running plays had been hammering to the inside with Triplett and Webster. That was a part of the plot.

Said Howell, "We would run through the middle mostly, to bring the defense in tighter. By then we figured we would have them set up for this wide play." The deception worked.

Conerly took the ball from Wietecha and faked a hand-off to Triplett, the fullback diving over left guard. His action caused the Eagle right end to close to the inside and the trap was set. As Rosey Brown swung wide to the left outside, Conerly quickly pitched the ball underhanded to Gifford running laterally to his left. "Go Ro," shouted Gifford to Brown.

Rote had screened the linebacker out of the play and Brown was bearing down on the defensive halfback as Gifford turned up field. The Philadelphia line, charging at the Triplett fake, could offer no pursuit. Brown made a key block on the halfback and Gifford realized 37 yards on the play before being caught from behind at the Eagle 20.

It was like Lombardi said: "He [Gifford] has a faster pickup going through a hole than anybody around. But his burst is good for only 20 yards. Fifty backs can outrun him over a long stretch."

Howell said once, "Frank did get caught a lot from behind after a long run. But he made a lot of yards just the same and we were grateful. If that team had had a real speed merchant on it, a game buster like Homer Jones of today, there's no telling what it could have done."

Following the weak side pitch play, the Giants slugged down to the Eagle goal, Webster scoring from the one.

Conerly and Gifford collaborated on another big

play for the Giants' second and last touchdown. Harland Svare blocked a punt by Adrian Burk, the Eagle quarterback, and the Giants had the ball on the Philadelphia 20. Conerly struck quickly. He faked once to Triplett and once more to Webster as Gifford ran to the end zone. Then Charley stepped back and floated a soft pass to Gifford who was under the cross bar between two defenders. Touchdown!

"It was the kind of a pass that belongs in a museum," said Gifford.

CHAPTER SEVEN

An embargo was placed on the exchange of films in the National Football League during the 1950's, an embargo continually broken by the smarter coaches who realized that studying the game films of an upcoming opponent was far better than paper-and-pencil reports written up by a scout in the press box.

The prohibition against films seemed to have come from some of the older, conservative and perhaps lazy coaches who were at the job only six months a year and did not wish to take on the work load of film study. But to people like Vince Lombardi, the offensive coach of the Giants, and Sid Gillman, head coach of the Los Angeles Rams, theirs was a lifetime profession. They aspired to excellence and they were willing to work hard at film study or any other element that would help their teams to win.

So the bootlegging of films began. The Rams would have a film of their game a month before against the Bears. The Giants were soon to play the Bears. Gillman would air mail the Rams-Bears game movie to Lombardi and a couple of weeks later a Giants-Eagles film would be dispatched to Los Angeles because the Rams were about to meet Philadelphia. This was far from the only exchange within the league.

Gillman, who had coached one year at West Point with Lombardi, certainly did not care. He would give anyone but his enemies any Ram film they wanted. The Giants felt the same way.

"It was ridiculous," said Gifford. "Football is the kind of game where the more you know about your opponent the better you will play on Sunday. Two well-coached, well-prepared teams will give a better performance for the fans.

"Vinnie Lombardi lived in New Jersey. We used to go over to his house at night after practice, Kyle and myself, Charley, maybe one or two others. We would watch the films he had sneaked from Gillman. We had some great sessions and we all learned a lot of football. Lombardi had been in the league three years by this time and he was getting sharper all the time. He knew what would go and what wouldn't go.

"We would put in a play for a team on one Sunday and then change it slightly so it started out looking exactly the same for the next game the following Sunday. Let's say it was a dive play with Triplett hitting into the six hole. The next week it would be the same except Charley would keep the ball and throw me a quick pass on the outside.

"That may seem old hat now. Everybody does things like that and the defenses have gotten a lot sharper. But back in those days it wasn't so common. Defenses were a lot easier to fool. And we fooled them."

For their sixth game of the 1956 season the Giants went out to Pittsburgh where the team for years has had a hard time. The visitors were favored by 10 points and there were 31,240 people in the stands at Forbes Field, the old baseball park.

Although the Steelers were a crippled team they almost won because the Giants played so poorly. There were six fumbles, three by each team with the other side recovering two. Fran Rogel, Pittsburgh's leading running back, fumbled first and Bill Svoboda recovered for the Giants at the Steeler 25.

Don Heinrich passed 15 yards to Bob Schnelker, the big but not so speedy end who played behind Rote and MacAfee. Heinrich then passed nine yards to Gifford to the one and Webster scored from there. Later Agajanian kicked a 32-yard field goal with 16 seconds left in the first half to give New York a 10-0 lead.

Rogel fumbled again and the Giants recovered at the Steeler 27. The attack moved to the end zone but Gifford fumbled at the one and the scoring opportunity was lost.

Fumbling is the woe of the running back's existence. In his time, Gifford dropped his share.

In his first two seasons with the Giants he irritated Steve Owen by carrying the ball loosely with one hand, like a college hot shot. "I guess it was carelessness on my part," said Gifford. "But I tried and I got better. It looked like I was fumbling more than I really was. It's something you can't think too much about because then you'll get tight and get worse. After you've fumbled, the best attitude is to forget it and look ahead to your next chance. Never think back or you're lost."

Against the Steelers Gifford fumbled again on the third play following the second-half kick-off. This time he was near his own goal and Ford of Pittsburgh recovered on the New York seven. Svoboda then saved the occasion by intercepting Ted Marchibroda's pass in the end zone for a touchback. Despite his fumbles, Gifford was the team's leading rusher, gaining 65 yards that day on 17 carries.

In the second half the New York defense held just often enough to preserve the victory. The Giants' second touchdown came on a clutch play, fourth down and three yards to go. Conerly faked to Webster on a dive play to freeze the defense and then quickly passed to Rote in the end zone.

Late in the game Gifford was a dispassionate onlooker when Lowell Perry, the Steelers' fine rookie end, was carried from the field on a stretcher. Perry, who weighed 190, had been tackled by Rosey Grier, all 290 pounds of him. The Steeler athlete had a dislocated hip and a broken pelvis. His promising career was over after six games.

"No one likes to see somebody get hurt," said Gifford. "But it's a part of football. After a while you just have to accept the fact that people are going to get hurt."

The Giants in that season of 1956 were fortunate.

They had no major injuries. "If we had," said Howell, "we were so thin we might not have won."

The following Sunday the Cardinals, who remained tied with the Giants for first place, came into the Yankee Stadium for a showdown game. Because the Browns had done so poorly, it appeared that the winner would go on to become the eastern champion.

New York was aroused. There was a crowd of 62,410 on hand, the second largest gathering ever to see the Giants play at home. The total had been exceeded back in 1925 at the Polo Grounds when a mob estimated at 70,000 came out to see Red Grange play for the Chicago Bears against the Giants for the first time.

Against the Cardinals, the Giants were champions. They won, 23-10, as both offense and defense played well. Gifford? In the big game, he produced the big plays.

The Cardinals had two fine defensive halfbacks, Dick (Night Train) Lane on the Giants' right and Jimmy Hill on their left. The Giants chose Hill as the lesser of two evils and stayed away from Lane, which was common practice in the N.F.L. for over a decade.

Early in the game Andy Robustelli blocked a punt by Dave Mann but Mann recovered the football in the end zone. This was a safety and gave the Giants two points. Heinrich then took his team 42 yards in 10 plays for a score, the latter coming on a six-yard pass to MacAfee.

Pat Summerall, later to become a famous Giant, kicked a field goal for the Cardinals and they trailed, 9-3. Ollie Matson was working hard but the Giants, especially Huff, were all over him and he wound up with merely 43 yards rushing in 13 carries.

Minor injuries had brought about three replacements in the New York defense. Jimmy Patton took over for Herb Rich at safety and remained in the starting lineup for ten years. Cliff Livingston replaced Svoboda, the defensive captain, at left linebacker and Jim Katcavage, a rookie, filled in for Dick Modzelewski at right tackle. Livingston and Katcavage too were to become longtime regulars on later teams.

Patton was small but wiry and he liked to come up and hit the big fullbacks such as Matson and Jim Brown head first. Landry, who wanted to keep him in the lineup, tried to discourage Patton. He told Patton that it would be all right with his coach if Jimmy let the backs go by and then tackled them from behind rather than hitting straight ahead. But Patton never did change his style and he was seldom injured.

With Conerly in the game, the Giants went ahead, 16-3. The supremely confident Gifford thought he could handle Hill and told Conerly so. Frank went to the outside, gained a step on Hill and caught a 30-yard pass. Hill made the tackle but it was not a good shot and Gifford failed to go down. He stumbled, broke free and headed for the goal line. Woodley Lewis eventually tackled him at the 12 but it was a 48-yard play. Webster then scored the touchdown.

Conerly and Gifford were not through. From the solid T, Gifford came out quickly on Hill again and this time clearly beat the defensive back at the sideline. The pass was on target and Gifford went all the way for a spectacular 43-yard touchdown play. That one wrapped up the game and the Giants were alone in first place with a 6-1 record.

Being in first place was heady wine for a team unaccustomed to such stature. The next Sunday, in Washington, the Giants were awful. They lost to the Redskins who came up with a hot quarterback in Al Dorow. The score was 33-7 and the New York winning streak of five became a memory.

But the Cardinals lost to Pittsburgh on the same day so the Giants' one game lead held. The Redskins by now were something of a threat. With Dorow in command of the offense, they had on successive Sundays beaten the Browns, the Cardinals, a good Detroit team and the Giants. They were 1½ games behind the Giants.

Gifford led the Giants in rushing with 63 yards but he spent the night after the game in St. Elizabeth's Hospital in New York. Howell and Lombardi were afraid they had lost their number one offensive player, the big-play man who more than anyone else had put the Giants in first place. At this point he was the only player in the league who had gained over 1,000 yards, 573 by rushing and 463 as a pass receiver.

Late in the game Gifford had been kneed in the back by Chuck Drazenovich, the Redskin linebacker. He left the field on a stretcher and left the Washington-New York train at Penn Station in the same fashion.

Recovery came quickly. By midweek Gifford was working out lightly at the stadium. Said he, "There's no pain at all when I run or go to catch a pass. The only time I feel pain is when I'm standing still."

The Giants had another big game ahead. The Chicago Bears were coming to New York for the first time in seven years and they were leading the western division with a 7-1 record. They had won seven in a row thanks to a powerful offense led by fullback Rick Casares, the league's leading ground gainer. Howell called the Bears "the best team in pro football," and he meant it.

Lombardi and Landry had the films from Gillman of the Rams' two losses to the Bears and they prepared carefully. The Giants were ready and so was Gifford.

Most long-term Giant fans remember this as one of the most important games in the annals of the team. New York would have won it easily, except for two big plays, as they whipped the Bears on offense and defense.

Casares went nowhere. The Bears' rushing game gained exactly 12 yards. George Halas, the Bears' owner, called the result "a clobbering." Halas could afford to be smug because his team got away with a tie rather than a defeat.

With their defense stopping Chicago cold, the Giants' offensive players could afford to be deliberate and play for ball control. They scored twice and Agajanian contributed a field goal for a 17-0 halftime lead. Heinrich did so well he was left in the game until only three minutes remained in the third period.

With their bread-and-butter offense frustrated, the Bears went for trickery. Bill McColl, the slotback, took the ball on a reverse from Ed Brown, the quarterback. The play looked like an end-around run until McColl stopped to pass. Way downfield Harlon Hill, the Bears' tall fast end from Florence State Teachers College in Alabama, was running as hard as he could.

McColl did not pass the football to Hill. He heaved it. With the ball airborne, Hill split the two safetymen, Patton and Tunnell, and when it came down he was five yards behind them. Hill caught the pass on the run and went on to the end zone, completing a 79-yard play.

The Bears added a field goal by George Blanda and late in the game they trailed, 17-10. But their offense was still making no progress.

With no options, Brown went for the bomb to Hill again. This time Patton was ready deep downfield. He was all over the Bear end inside the Giants' five-yard line when Brown's pass of 60 yards came down. Hill, his body on a horizontal plane, caught the ball with outstretched hands while falling with Patton on his back. He fell into the end zone for a touchdown and when Blanda kicked the conversion, the score was tied for good.

In later years Howell said, "It was a great catch, one of the greatest. And you can't fault Patton. He was there. The pass had to be perfect too. Later we tried to second-guess ourselves. It was so late in the game maybe we should have had a prevent defense in there, an extra defensive back for passes. But Landry didn't want to change things around. He had gone all season with this defense and it had held up well. We wouldn't have been there otherwise. Still it was a tough result for us to swallow after we had played so well. The offensive blocking, which hadn't been so good for three weeks, was just great."

The Cardinals had defeated Pittsburgh so the Giants'

lead was cut to half a game with three left to play.

In the Bears' game Gifford was steady if not spectacular. Halas, who had only a cursory knowledge of Gifford, was impressed. The man who had been around pro football since the National League was founded in 1920 said of Frank Gifford, "He's the best all-around back that's been in the league since Dutch Clark 20 years ago." Clark, who played for the Detroit Lions in the 1930's, was to become a charter member of pro football's Hall of Fame in 1963.

Added Halas, "An athlete doesn't reach his peak until he is four or five years out of college. Gifford had to beef up his potential."

Gifford concurred. "At first with the Giants," he said in 1957, "I was playing only with my legs. I had an incomplete map of the game in my head.

"It seems to me that there are three stages in the evolution of a ball carrier. In high school he learns where the play is going. In college he learns who is blocking for him. In pro football he learns what the defense is doing. He must visualize the play while he is running. He must know where everybody on the field is supposed to be so he can take advantage of a player out of position.

"This eventually is an instinctive reaction. It comes from a highly developed sense of awareness. You cultivate it by studying game movies.

"In the pros, football is not a muscle game as it is in college. Muscle is cancelled out. I wasted a couple of years because I didn't bear down hard enough mentally."

Speaking after he had retired as a player, Gifford

expanded on this theme. "The difference between success and failure, or not so much success," he said, "lies in the philosophy the player brings to the game. I didn't think my physical equipment was so much better than a lot of others'. It took me awhile before I realized that to be really successful I had to try harder, to study so as to squeeze everything out of my physical ability that there was to give. I worked at pro football, worked at it hard."

Lombardi concurred with Halas. Of his prize, he said in 1957, "Gifford has two intangibles that make him great—versatility and alertness. He gives opponents fits by keeping them off balance. What looks like a wide sweep can be an option play. His greatest value is spotting weaknesses. He and Rote are the smartest players I've ever seen for coming up with a bright idea to exploit a situation."

As December of 1956 came on, Gifford and the other Giants still had some exploiting to do.

CHAPTER EIGHT

"Charley didn't like what he saw and was trying to throw the ball away, throw it right through the end zone. It was first down so it didn't make any difference. But he didn't throw the ball hard enough. So I reached up and caught it—for a touchdown. We laughed about that."

The comments were Gifford's about a play that took place in the third period of the New York Giants-Washington Redskins game in Yankee Stadium before 46,351 spectators on December 2, 1956.

This game was Gifford's finest of that season and perhaps one of the best he ever played. The Giants won, 28-14, but the head coach, Jim Lee Howell, was not pleased. "It was a sloppy game," he said, "with more mistakes than a top game should have. But Gifford was outstanding."

Outstanding indeed. He tied an all-time Giant single-game record by scoring 18 points on three touchdowns. He also threw a pass for a fourth touchdown; gained 108 yards in 19 rushing attempts and caught six passes for 53 more yards. The Giants' running attack was so well balanced that this game marked the only time all season that any back gained more than 100 yards in an afternoon.

The game had a "must" character to it. Had the Giants lost and the Cardinals beaten Green Bay, New York would have dropped out of first place into a tie for second with Washington. The Giants were learning to rise to such occasions. When the day was over, and the fading Cardinals had lost to Green Bay, the New York lead was up to 1½ games with only two left to play.

The Redskins helped. They fumbled five times and New York recovered three. Four of their passes were intercepted, two by Sam Huff.

Up to this game one of Gifford's more lethal weapons, the option pass, had been all but dormant. The man whom Lombardi was to call "probably the best option pass-runner I ever saw," had tried three aerials, completing one with one intercepted.

The Giants' opening drive against Washington carried 81 yards in 11 plays. On the last play Don Heinrich made a belly fake to Triplett who hit into the left guard hole. Then Heinrich faked to Webster who was also crossing to the left. Heinrich's third move was to hand the football to Gifford going from left to right. The early play action of Triplett and Webster had caused the defense to react to its right, away from Gifford, or to freeze awaiting further developments.

Jack Stroud, the right guard, had pulled out as though to run interference to the left but had then reversed his field and gone to the right. He was a blocking shield for Gifford's supposed reverse sweep around right end.

Gifford moved 10 yards into the flat and, on the run, threw a pass over the head of Gary Lowe, the defending halfback moving up to tackle him. The pass went to Ken MacAfee in the end zone completing a fancy 29-yard touchdown play. It was this kind of unexpected play that endeared these Giants to their fans, who, like all fans, love razzle-dazzle football when it works.

"In our previous game against Washington," said Gifford, "we ran the same kind of play without the pass in it and it didn't work. So this time we put in the pass option. If Lowe had not come up, I would have run."

Howell, ever the perfectionist, admitted it was a pretty good play. "But Gifford almost gave it away," he said. "That pivot of his was so obvious when he reversed his direction at the start of the play I thought he had tipped it off for sure."

For openers, this was an effective effort. Joe Scudero of the Redskins fumbled the ensuing kick-off and it was the Giants' ball on the Washington six. The two guards, Stroud and Gerry Huth from Floyd Knobbs, Indiana, who was playing in place of Bill Austin, pulled out and swung to the right.

It was a power sweep with Gifford carrying. The

guards' blocks were there and Frank ran right over Roy Barni, the Washington defensive back, for touchdown No. 1.

The Giants led, 14-7, at halftime. In the third quarter the Conerly-Gifford team ran the "48 pitchout play" to the weak side, Gifford gaining 28 yards to the Washington 14 behind Rosey Brown's big block. From there, Gifford caught the pass Conerly was trying to throw away for touchdown No. 2.

Gifford merely came out of the backfield on this pass pattern and the Redskins made the mistake of trying to cover him with a 235-pound defensive end, Chet Ostrowski. It was no contest.

In the fourth quarter Conerly twice threw passes to Gifford that carried to the 11. Then Gifford took off on the sweep again and scored standing up. Touchdown No. 3. That put the Giants ahead, 28-7.

After his touchdowns Gifford was unperturbed, displaying none of the histrionics of the "hot dog," the show-off player. He merely handed the football to the nearest official and ran quietly to the sidelines. Scoring touchdowns had become routine for the man who made the big plays.

After this game Gifford was the toast of the town. "All week," he said, "wherever I went people were after me. I must have signed a thousand autographs. I felt like I was being discovered. Hell, I'd been around for five seasons. I kept thinking, 'Where were all you people before?' "

The Giants could have clinched their eastern title the next Sunday by beating the Cleveland Browns who had been eliminated from the race two weeks before. But they did not and Cleveland won a miserable game played in heavy rain. The score was 24-7 and Gifford typically had no memory of the afternoon when asked about it several years later.

"I only remember the games we won," he joked. There was little to remember as 27,707 fans, the smallest crowd of the season in New York, huddled under umbrellas. In the second period Conerly in the mud threw a careful, deliberate six-yard touchdown pass to Gifford to tie the score at 7-7. Two minutes later Lou Groza kicked a 41-yard field goal and away the Browns went.

Gifford banged a knee that day. He also caught six passes to make a season's total of 49, thus passing the Giant all-time record of 47 set by Bill Swiacki in 1947.

Swiacki had been an end and Gifford was a back. This was significant in the offensive evaluation within pro football. The Giants were pacesetters in utilizing backs as pass receivers. Fortunately they had in Webster and Gifford, if not in Triplett, backs who could run pass patterns ably, break open and catch the football. Conerly and Heinrich had four good receivers to throw to and this made a lot of offensive opportunities.

Said Howell, "When you send one or two backs out for passes you of course reduce the blocking protection you can give your quarterback, especially against blitzing linebackers. A lot of coaches told me they couldn't understand how we got away with sending out two backs on pass plays. They thought our quarterbacks should get killed. We mixed it up, kept two backs in most times and sometimes just one. We had smart players, like Wietecha. He knew how to pick up the blitzers. Our quarterback protection was good right through the season."

Figures substantiate this. Conerly and Heinrich lost fewer yards when thrown while attempting to pass than any other team's quarterbacks. The Giants figure was merely 34 yards while the league average was 165.

The loss to Cleveland left New York in a curious situation. The Cardinals, who had been the chief competition all season, also lost—to the Bears—and thus were eliminated from the eastern race. The one team still alive was Washington. The Redskins were one game behind the Giants and had a 6-4 record. The Giants' tie with the Bears was meaningless as the N.F.L. rules discount deadlocks. They are thrown out of the standings.

The Giants had one game to play but the Redskins had two remaining. New York could lose the eastern title by dropping the final game to Philadelphia provided Washington beat Pittsburgh and Baltimore in its last two contests. If Washington lost once, however, the title was the Giants'.

Howell was asked how he felt about "backing into the title," meaning if Washington lost. "I'll back in, slide in, sneak in," he replied. "Any way to get it over with." The Giants had not won an eastern division title in 10 years and the anxiety was intense.

It ended with a Saturday game in Philadelphia's Connie Mack Stadium against the Eagles. A crowd of only 16,562 was present to see the Giants win their precious title. The Eagles offered only mild opposition and the final score was 21-7. It was the first time the Giants had won in Philadelphia since 1952.

Don Heinrich went all the way at quarterback with Charley Conerly on the bench, but available. Conerly's foot had been stepped on the week before; the Eagles did not offer too much resistance, especially on offense, and Heinrich not only started well but finished well. Said Howell many years later, "I figured we could win the game and I didn't want Charley to get hurt."

The Giants made two long drives in the first and second quarters, which decided this game and the eastern championship. At the Eagle 17-yard line, Gifford sensed that the weak side pitchout play would go and told Heinrich so. It worked, Heinrich faking to Triplett going to the strong side and then pitching the football underhanded to Gifford. Rosey Brown peeled off for the downfield block; Alex Webster added a block of his own in the secondary, and Gifford made his way down to the six where he was knocked out of bounds and into the left field wall of the stadium.

The Giants came right back and appeared to be repeating the play. But this time Gifford pulled up and threw a pass to Kyle Rote in the end zone for a touchdown. Gifford was such a threat in the early forming of this play that the Eagle defenders instinctively came up to meet him. As a result Rote found himself wide open behind Bibbles Bawel, the Eagle defensive back. This play ended a 65-yard drive.

Later in the second quarter a New York drive of 61 yards concluded with Gifford scoring from the 10 on the familiar power sweep to the right or strong side. Stroud and Gerry Huth were the pulling guards who did the blocking. Gifford, who never claimed to have brute power, dragged Eddie Bell, the Philadelphia safety, across the goal.

The Eagles were out of it after those two touchdowns as the Giants continued to play a disciplined, ball-control kind of game. Webster carried 12 times to gain 70 yards, Gifford 11 for 62 yards and Triplett 6 for 45 yards. It was a typical balanced performance.

The eastern title, the first in 10 years, was the Giants' ninth in the 23 years since the National Football League had been split into two divisions, eastern and western. For Coach Howell, a championship came in his third season as the head man. But Jim Lee was more concerned about the impending arrival of his new baby and in the locker room he went right to the telephone to call home.

The locker room was relatively subdued for a group of athletes who, for the most part, had never before won anything as significant. There was no domestic champagne being flung around the room as so often happens in similar situations. "We were delighted," said Gifford, "but we didn't go for that kind of thing. It wasn't the Maras' style and besides we had another game to go."

The Bears had staggered a bit after their tie game against the Giants. The following Sunday they were smashed by the Lions at Detroit, 42-10, and dropped half a game behind those Lions in the western division standings.

Under Buddy Parker, the laconic, permissive coach, the Lions had been a force to contend with since 1951, winning the western division title in 1952, 1953 and

1954. They had a disastrous season in 1955, dropping to last place, but came back strong in 1956, winning their first six games. Parker may have been the coach but this team in truth belonged to Bobby Layne, as did every team that Bobby played for. Layne, the quarterback, was a competitor in every sense and he set standards and made demands of his teammates to which they had to respond.

On December 9, the Lions defeated Pittsburgh and the Bears beat the Chicago Cardinals so that Detroit continued to lead in the standings by half a game. The Bears' record was 8-2-1, the Lions' 9-2, with one game to go. The schedule provided the perfect climax. The two were to play at Wrigley Field in Chicago on December 16. The Bears had to win. A tie or a victory would give the western title to the Lions.

It was a fierce, bruising game, full of fights. Ed Meadows, the Bears' defensive end, hit Layne so hard with his forearm and elbow that the Detroit quarterback left the field with a concussion. Charges of "dirty football" echoed through the land for some weeks afterwards.

But the Bears won, 39-21. It was their first division title in 10 years and they ended the dynasty of the Lions as the Giants had done to the Cleveland Browns. The Lions and Browns did come back in 1957 to play for the league championship but in following seasons they were merely contenders as the balance of power in the N.F.L. shifted to Baltimore followed by Green Bay in the west, and to New York in the east.

Both the Bears and the Giants had two weeks to think about one another before the championship game.

It was scheduled for Yankee Stadium on December 30.

Meanwhile there was time for reflection. Gifford's statistics, like all statistics, failed to reflect the value of the big plays which this 26-year-old halfback had contributed to his team all season. Still, those numbers were impressive enough.

He had gained 1,422 total yards, 819 rushing and 603 receiving passes. In the overall league statistics he was in the top five in both categories—a distinction no one had ever achieved before.

Gifford had scored nine touchdowns, passed for two others, kicked eight extra points and one field goal.

The Newspaper Enterprise Association annually runs a poll of the players, asking them to vote for an all-star team and also to select the one man they consider to be the best performer of the year. The winner receives the Jim Thorpe Memorial Trophy named after the great Indian athlete who was pro football's first hero.

For 1956, Gifford won this significant award. The voting was close. Gifford received 100 votes. Layne, who had taken the Lions almost all the way, gained 97. Harlon Hill, the Bears' spectacular end, had 78; Tobin Rote, a superb quarterback for a losing Green Bay team, 65, and Matson of the Chicago Cardinals, 51.

Gifford was extremely proud of this trophy. In previous years he had gone back to Bakersfield to visit after the football seasons. "I'd see somebody on the street I knew," said Gifford. "They would say, 'Gee, where have you been?' I'd say, 'In New York.' And they would say, 'Doing what?' "

Now they all knew what.

CHAPTER NINE

❦❦❦

It would be stretching the point a bit but not much to say that the New York Giants had the 1956 championship of the National Football League in their grasp after the very first play. George Blanda of the Chicago Bears kicked off and Gene Filipski, Frank Gifford's substitute, took the ball on New York's eight. He was already running, shod in high-topped white gym sneakers as were all the other Giants.

Filipski did not stop running until he had gone down the left side all the way to the Bears' 39-yard line. It had been a 53-yard kick-off return which, short of a touchdown, was the best possible way to open a championship game. Such a quick thrust had to upset the Bears, to chew at their confidence, to put doubt about winning in their minds.

Said Vince Lombardi, "I knew we were on our way with Filipski's kick-off return."

The Giants were on their way. After the first 30 minutes of play they were ahead, 34-7, and the Bears, who had been favored by 3 points, were demoralized. The final score was 47-7. The only comparably decisive results in 33 years of N.F.L. championships were the Bear's famous 73-0 defeat of the Washington Redskins in 1940, the Browns' 56-10 conquest of the Lions in 1954, and the Lions' 59-14 skunking of the Browns in 1957.

The temperature that day in Yankee Stadium was 20 degrees and there was a stiff breeze blowing. To many it seemed as cold as minus 20. The *Herald Tribune* that morning had seemed quite certain that the contest, the first for a league title in New York in ten years and the first ever at Yankee Stadium, would draw a crowd of 68,000. There were 64,800 seats available plus plenty of standing room.

The *Herald Tribune* estimate was too generous. The crowd came to 56,836, considerably short of capacity, and the weather was blamed. Wide enthusiasm for pro football was only beginning in New York that season and there was not enough of it to fill the stadium regardless of the weather. By 1962, when the Giants played Green Bay for the league title, the Stadium was packed and every ticket was at a premium even though the temperature was lower and the wind considerably more brisk.

Thirty-two years before these teams had met at the Polo Grounds for the same championship. The field was frozen hard. Both sides slipped and slid until an emergency call by the Giants brought forth two dozen pairs of basketball sneakers, obtained from the Manhattan College gymnasium while the game was under way.

The Giants were shod with sneakers during the half-time intermission and their traction on a surface as hard as a basketball court immediately improved. In the second half, after trailing 13-3, they buried the Bears and won the game, 30-13.

In the 1956 championship event, all the Giants save the kickers, Chandler and Agajanian, wore sneakers from the start. Most of the Bears had them too but something was wrong. Said Paddy Driscoll, coach of the Bears, "They [the Giants] seemed to move better than we did. It looked like their sneakers had thicker soles. Ours were pretty old."

The quality of the sneakers or even their absence in this game did not make as significant a difference as in 1934. The Giants were destined to win, it seemed, even if they had been equipped with lead galoshes.

With first down at the Bears' 38, the Giants ran two running plays that gained two yards. Then Gifford struck. He caught a pass at the right sideline from Heinrich for 21 yards to the Chicago 17 and on the next play Mel Triplett ran all the way to the end zone for the first of six New York touchdowns.

On the pass play, Gifford was flanked to the right. The defensive halfback covering him was J. C. Caroline, a fine athlete but a rookie and nervous. "I knew he would be nervous," said Gifford. "From the earlier game we played them, I knew I could fake him. We had decided to throw our first pass at him."

The pass pattern was an "acute out," calling for Gifford to take Caroline deep to the outside, then come back toward the scrimmage line. This pattern virtually insured a completion provided the pass was thrown well, but the gain was a relatively small one.

Heinrich, the quarterback, casually rolled out to his right and flung the ball downfield with abandon. Gifford had no chance to come back toward the scrimmage line. Instead he had to compete with Caroline for the ball as both went up to catch it. "I gave him a shot," said Gifford, meaning hip action and an elbow in Caroline's chest. The Giant, not the Bear, came down with the ball and Gifford was gone, flying down the sideline to the 17 where he was knocked out of bounds.

This play had Gifford's trademark all over it. First, there was study—study of Caroline and an estimate of his weaknesses from game films plus the experience of the prior game against the Bears. Second was the cleverness of Gifford and certainly Lombardi to agree to a "safe" pattern, meaning the "acute out" with the turnback feature in it. Third, Gifford's pure physical ability enabled him to get to the football after Heinrich had all but wrecked the play by throwing the ball deep. Fourth, there was Gifford's competitiveness when he and Caroline went up for the catch together. Frank was determined to take the ball down, rather than let Caroline have it.

After Triplett, a stand-up runner with an uneven style described by Howell as "buck and snort," had smashed to the end zone for the first touchdown, Agajanian kicked the conversion and New York led, 7-0.

The Giants kicked off and two plays later Rick

Casares, the Bears' fullback, fumbled. Andy Robustelli recovered on the Chicago 15-yard line. But the Giants could make only five yards in three plays and on fourth down 38-year-old Agajanian kicked a 17-yard field goal. New York led, 10-0.

Jimmy Patton, the safetyman, intercepted a pass thrown by Ed Brown, the Bears' quarterback, at the Giants' 36-yard line. Behind a crushing block by Swede Svare, little Patton sprinted down to the Bears' 36. The Giants were turned back for three downs and on fourth down Agajanian made good on a 43-yard field goal attempt, the longest field goal of the season for the New York team.

Late in the first period and behind, 13-0, the Bears gambled on fourth down at their 44-yard line. They needed a yard for a first down to get rolling. Caroline, who played on both offense and defense that afternoon, was elected to run outside tackle. He never reached the scrimmage line as Emlen Tunnell, the safetyman, sprinted into the Bears' backfield to nail Caroline for a one-yard loss.

It was the Giants' ball. In six plays they drove to the Chicago goal, Webster scoring from the 3. With the second period still young, the New York lead was 20-0.

Tunnell fumbled a punt by Brown at the Giants' 25 where John Mellekas recovered for Chicago. Five plays later Casares drove for a touchdown from seven yards out, and the New York lead was cut to 20-7.

The Giants were not worried. They drove 72 yards in five quick plays. The key plays were a 50-yard pass from Conerly, who had succeeded Heinrich, to Webster; a 20-yard run by Triplett, and a one-yard plunge by Webster for the touchdown. The scoreboard read New York 27, Chicago 7.

The home side now had tremendous drive and the Giants were all over the Bears. Ed Brown could not get a punt away in the end zone with four Giants charging down on him. Ray Beck blocked the punt and Henry Moore, a rookie defensive back for New York, recovered it in the end zone for another touchdown. The second period closed with the Bears behind, 34-7.

The final two periods were rather a drag. It is terrible to suspect that a team has quit, has given up, but the thought was there with regard to the Bears.

There was no letup among the Giants. Conerly threw a pass to Gifford over the middle that went for 67 yards and set up one more touchdown. The confidence that these two athletes and friends shared in one another was evident on this play. Gifford broke the pass pattern, going to the inside instead of the outside when he was crowded by a linebacker and could not break free. Conerly sensed this and hit Gifford over the middle.

"I got away with murder because I crossed up my quarterback," said Gifford. "If Conerly had thrown to the spot called for in the pass play, there would have been a sure interception. I was hoping Charley would realize my situation and was pretty confident that he would."

Gifford, the not-so-speedy demon, was caught from behind by Stan Wallace, the Bears' safetyman, at the Chicago 9. It had been one of the longest plays of the year for the Giants.

From the 9, Conerly threw a square-in pass to Rote

for a touchdown. Kyle was framed by the goal posts as he leaped to catch the ball directly under the cross bar. The action was captured by news photographers and the composition was perfect. So was the symbolism. The Bears were dead.

The Bears were helpless on offense and Brown, the league-leading quarterback, was carried off the field on a stretcher. He had been knocked cold on a tackle by Walt Yowarsky, the New York left end.

In the fourth period the Giants made their last move, a quick four-play 62-yard drive to a sixth touchdown. Gifford scored.

Frank swung out of the backfield from the solid T formation and ran for the left corner. (The play had begun on the Chicago 14.) Joe Fortunato, the Bears' right linebacker, went with him to cover. Conerly threw a perfect pass which Gifford caught effortlessly by turning his upper body to the right and catching the ball at his right hip. Fortunato, covering on the outside of his man, had no chance at the ball.

That touchdown and a conversion by Agajanian brought the score to 47-7 and the game was soon over.

The Giants were jubilant and so were the owners, the three Mara men, T.J., Jack and Well. Although the Giants had won a number of eastern division titles—nine since 1933—they had won the league championship only twice before, in 1934 against the Bears and in 1938 over the Green Bay Packers.

"We went down to Toots Shor's after the game," recalled Gifford, "and had a party." Toots Shor's is the well-known sports restaurant on West 52nd Street in Manhattan and the proprietor, after whom the place is named, has been a Giants' fan for many years. "It was a pretty good party," continued Gifford. "Nothing too wild or rowdy. We kept telling each other, 'We're champions.' It took a while to sink in."

The material evidence came several weeks later when each of the Giants received from league headquarters a check for $3,799.19, the amount of the winning players' share out of the gate receipts and the television money. That was a record share at the time and quite a contrast from the $621 each Giant had received for winning the title over the Bears in 1934.

There was one more game remaining for seven of the Giants, the annual Pro Bowl contest in Los Angeles on January 13, 1957, between the best players of the western and eastern divisions. There were seven Giants on the East squad that lost to the West, 19-10. They were Andy Robustelli, Emlen Tunnell and Rosey Grier on defense, Rosey Brown, Kyle Rote, Charley Conerly and of course Frank Gifford for offense. After all he was player of the year.

CHAPTER TEN

On Sunday morning, November 20, 1960, Frank Gifford drove from his home in Scarsdale, New York, to Yankee Stadium in the Bronx. He was going to work. The Giants had a game with the Philadelphia Eagles that afternoon, a big game.

Gifford had a companion in the car with him. It was Bob Karpe. They had been friends for a long time. Karpe played with Frank on the Bakersfield High School juggernaut of 1947 and later went to college at Berkeley where he starred on the good University of California teams of the era. One of his college teammates had been Les Richter, the all-America linebacker.

In the years after college the three of them—Gifford, Karpe and Richter—had formed a partnership in Bakersfield and acquired various real estate properties, some undeveloped and others, such as an apartment house, producing income. It was a partnership that had just begun in 1960 but the potential was there and certainly recognized by Karpe.

Gifford and he discussed how much longer Frank might play pro football. Frank was then 30 and in his ninth pro season. He knew, and so did Karpe, that the end of an outstanding football career was in sight if not near at hand.

"I had been thinking about retiring," said Frank, "and going back to Bakersfield. But I hadn't made up my mind. I remember saying to Bob as we neared the stadium that if I got hurt the decision might come sooner.

"Later on we talked about that ride and what I said about injury. He got a big kick out of that after what happened."

With Norm Van Brocklin, the smart quarterback who got the most out of his teammates, the Eagles were flying high. In three seasons, 1958-1959-1960, Coach Buck Shaw and Van Brocklin had taken the Eagles from the bottom of the league standings into a position as a championship contender.

Going into the game against the Giants, the Eagles had won six out of seven games. They held a 1½ game lead over New York and so the Giants had to win to stay close to Philadelphia. This was to be the eighth game of the season with four more to go.

The Giants started out very well. Harlan Svare was the new defensive coach in place of Tom Landry who had become head coach of the expansion team, the Dallas Cowboys. For the Eagles and Van Brocklin, Svare had decided to depart from the usually conservative Giants' defensive strategy and go for a full blitz against the Eagle quarterback.

For the first half at least, the blitz worked. Van Brocklin could never quite locate Sam Huff, the middle linebacker, and "The Dutchman" frequently found himself having to throw the ball away. After two periods the Giants were ahead, 10-3.

All good quarterbacks like to be blitzed. The incoming linebackers leave great gaps in the defensive pass coverage as they gamble, their aim being to drop the passer before he can get the ball in the air.

The blitz was just beginning to be exploited that season and Van Brocklin, in the second half against the Giants, gave a masterful demonstration of how a smart quarterback can destroy it. On the Eagles' first offensive series of the second half, Van Brocklin sensed on third down that the Giants were coming with the blitz. Huff certainly was coming. The Dutchman quickly dropped back a few steps and flipped a little pass over the charging Huff's helmet into the hands of Ted Dean, the Philadelphia fullback. Dean caught the ball and raced downfield for a long gain that led to the Eagles' first touchdown. That play marked the beginning of the end for the Giants who were to lose the game, 17-10, and all but drop out of championship contention.

Late in the game the Giants' offense was struggling to gain a tying touchdown. Charley Conerly threw a short pass to Gifford, who had been flanked to the right. Gifford turned to his right, or to the outside, to catch the pass and had to stop to wait for the ball.

Chuck Bednarik was the brilliant middle linebacker for the Eagles, the one star on a defensive unit that was otherwise undistinguished.

Bednarik, a big man, age 35 and in his twelfth pro season, had an undeserved "bad guy" reputation. He was a clean but hard football player and always had been.

He came over quickly to tackle Gifford from the latter's blind side. Because he had to hold up to wait for the football, Frank was a stationary target. The ball came, Frank caught it and then Bednarik struck. In these situations the tacklers hit their targets just as hard as they can. That is what football is all about.

Gifford went down, his helmet hitting the hard cold ground. He had been knocked unconscious and the ball dropped out of his hands. The fumble was recovered by the Eagles. Bednarik got up but Gifford did not.

Bednarik was jubilant. He danced about, waving his arms in glee. The partisan crowd, seeing the Giants' hero motionless on the ground, let go with roars of anger.

Bednarik was later to explain over and over that he had jumped about in pleasure not because Gifford remained on the ground but because the Eagles had recovered the fumble, thus ending a Giant thrust and all but assuring a victory for Philadelphia. But Bednarik's actions were misunderstood.

Gifford was taken to the locker room on a stretcher. He remained unconscious while Dr. Francis Sweeney, the team physician, hovered over him. A member of the stadium security force had earlier been taken to the locker room and died there of heart failure. But Gifford lived. He regained consciousness a few yards away from the special policeman and soon was taken to St. Elizabeth's Hospital.

He had a concussion, but it was not especially serious, and the athlete stayed only a few days in the hospital before going home. There was no consideration of his playing football again that season.

Back in Philadelphia, the contrite Bednarik wired Gifford, sent get-well cards, letters, flowers. "I didn't answer him," said Gifford later. "The Giants were playing the Eagles again the next Sunday and I wanted him to stay subdued."

The Giants lost that game too and the Eagles went on to win the eastern title and then beat the Green Bay Packers for the league championship.

The furor over the Gifford injury continued in New York. Said Gifford later, "Bednarik's tackle was a legal one. The occasion was blown out of proportion because it happened to me and the game was important. Any concussion can be serious. But I never felt I was knocking at death's door even though I may kid about it now."

"Because it happened to me." Gifford was fully aware of his stature as the hero. If Bednarik had leveled another, lesser Giant, the incident would have been far less significant.

Gifford went on to talk about injuries. "I don't think football," he said, "is half as dangerous as it's made out to be. I'd like to see my two sons play if they want to. It's good for boys to take part in a competitive, rough sport. They'll have to live that way so they might as well start young."

On February 10, 1961, Gifford announced his retirement from active duty in pro football. The motivation, he said, was a long-term radio contract from the Columbia Broadcasting System for which Frank had done a five-minute sports show for several years. No one could quite believe that a radio sports show would lure a player of Gifford's stature into retirement. Many suspected the Bednarik incident was at the heart of the matter. Arthur Daley of *The New York Times* wrote that if the Bednarik incident was not the prime factor it certainly "hastened" the retirement of Frank Gifford.

Daley, in writing an obituary on Gifford-the-athlete, added that Frank was "so strikingly good looking in a wholesome way that he has acted in movies and on television. He doubled as an advertising model. He was a glib, attractive personality as a TV commentator. He wrote a sports column for his hometown newspaper. He is married to the campus beauty queen." These matters were largely accurate.

Gifford, however, had not quit football because of a hard tackle by an opponent. He rather resented the implication but had the good taste and judgement to be quiet about it.

Instead, he was seeking for himself, his wife and three children more security than a life of football could offer. Gifford, who had not enjoyed the comforts of wealth in his early years, respected money and has always wished to acquire a large share for himself.

After the 1956 season, his golden year, Gifford received and took many opportunities to spread his fame and earn some extra money. Radio was one, "writing" a sports column (which somebody else wrote) for the New York *Journal American* was another. Then there were advertising endorsements, paid appearances and dinner speeches—the usual but temporary round of affairs for the famous athlete.

Said Gifford in 1957, "A professional athlete can't learn a trade because no one will hire him for six months. That's why I am batting off in all directions. Hell, I don't even know how to pump gas or draw beer."

This was not quite true. When he left Southern California in 1952, Gifford was short credits for a degree. But he went back for three spring semesters, taking night courses, until 1955 when he received a degree in industrial management. If Gifford did not know how to pump gas or draw beer he certainly had the equipment with which to learn in a hurry.

As a writer for radio or for newspapers, Gifford had competence together with some imagination. One time he was comparing pro football to college football and he hit upon this new approach. "Pro ball is much noisier . . . loud grunts and laborious sneezes as guys hit one another. In college there is a muffled thud when the center snaps the ball. In the pro's, it is a smart smack like the crack of a whip." Not bad, for an athlete.

With retirement came eulogy. There was much to recall, even after the golden year of 1956.

In 1957 the Cleveland Browns staged a recovery and won the eastern division title with the Giants second, 2½ games back. Gifford had another good season (528 yards gained rushing, 41 passes caught), but his team did not win. That left Frank puzzled and somewhat embittered.

In a 1958 interview he said, "In 1956 I had a great season. It was due mostly to my teammates but I got the credit. The Giants won. I was on top of the world. Well, last year I think I was as good as in 1956. But nothing happened. I mean I got nowhere from what I did in 1957 and I have a wife and three children to consider.

"That's why I say, 'what do you do for an encore?' In pro football you have to keep topping your best effort. Being merely as good as you were the year before apparently isn't good enough."

Gifford then went off and signed a long-term movie contract with Warner Brothers and planned to play only one more year. It has never been established how good or bad Gifford was as an actor but there is suspicion he was far better as a halfback. Warner Brothers did little with their new property and Gifford broke the contract in 1959 when he did not drop out of football as the pact required. Warners suspended him, grumbled, threatened suit and then forgot all about it.

The 1958 season will never be forgotten by Giant fans. As Gifford put it, "The whole season was thrilling. We didn't have much of a ball club that year but we kept winning games, four or five in the closing minutes."

The Giants in the last game of the season had to beat Cleveland to tie the Browns for first place in the East. They did this in the snow when Pat Summerall kicked a field goal with three minutes left. It covered 49 yards against the wind.

In a division play-off game a week later the Giants shut out the Browns and their star fullback, Jim Brown. The score was 10-0.

The New York touchdown came on a trick play near the Cleveland goal line, one that Gifford had stumped for. It was a double reverse, Conerly to Webster to Gifford which was not so unusual. But on the end of the planned play Gifford pitched the ball out wide to the trailing Conerly and the Browns were bewildered as Charley just made it in to the end zone. Since quarterbacks are valuable commodities, few pitchouts are thrown to them especially when they are as slow afoot as 37-year-old Conerly.

"That was so like Gifford," recalled Jim Lee Howell. "Frank thought so much of Conerly, he wanted that play so Charley could get a little of the glory."

In the championship game, the Giants lost to the Baltimore Colts, 23-17, after eight minutes and 15 seconds of a fifth "sudden death" overtime period had been played. It was widely hailed as the greatest football game ever played.

Gifford disagreed. "The 'best ever played'? I can't agree with that. We were tired out. We didn't have much left."

His opinion might have been flavored by his performance, which was not up to his usual standard of excellence in key games. Although Gifford did score the touchdown which helped the Giants to go ahead 17-14 in the fourth period, he also fumbled twice in the second period and Baltimore recovered both. The Colts scored two touchdowns after the fumble recoveries.

Gifford also failed to gain a yard for a first down in the last two minutes of the fourth period when the Giants were protecting their 17-14 lead. But this was not entirely his fault. The Giants chose to run their power sweep to the strong side against Gino Marchetti, the best defensive end in pro football, and Big Daddy Lipscomb, the huge tackle. The two Colt linemen tackled

Gifford on the third down play and Marchetti hit with enough force to break his own ankle.

In 1959 the Giants again won the eastern title, for the third time in four seasons. Gifford led the Giants in both rushing and pass receiving, ranking 13th and seventh respectively in the league individual standings. He continued to earn his pay for New York. Baltimore beat the Giants handily this time in the championship game, 31-16.

Gifford's retirement, following the 1960 season, lasted one year, a year in which he served as a scout of future opponents for the Giants providing "perceptive, illuminating espionage information." There was a new head coach, Allie Sherman. Jim Lee Howell had retired to become director of player personnel, a safer, more tranquil job. By the admission of both, Howell had driven Gifford hard. For example, Howell once said of Gifford's rookie year, "The first few weeks I didn't think Gifford was putting out, he had such a smooth, easy stride. The boys nicknamed him 'Tippy Toes.' It looked like loafing. We might have released him if he hadn't been our first draft choice."

Later Howell was to add, "Gifford thought he was trying hard but he really didn't know what it was to bust his gut for an extra yard until Alex Webster joined the team in 1955."

Sherman's technique was different. He preferred to cajole his stars, asking them to accept him as an equal and a friend, although he could be quite impatient and sharp with those who were in no way star performers.

Perhaps it was the prospect of playing for his old pal Allie that brought Gifford back to pro football and the

Giants for the 1962 season. It's hard to say. The official line was vague. Gifford said he came back "for many reasons. First, I love the game. Possibly I made a mistake in leaving. Second, I couldn't get tickets."

He was being flippant. The Giants by this time were sold out for every home game and 50,000 season tickets were snapped up in advance.

Maxine Gifford possibly said it best. "When someone enjoys football as much as Frank does, there's no good reason why he shouldn't play as long as he can and wants to."

There were some more years ahead for Frank Gifford, football player. And they were good years, the gleam in the gold never diminishing.

CHAPTER ELEVEN

On October 27, 1963, the New York Giants, who were then the monarchs of the eastern division of the National Football League, came to Cleveland to play their rivals, the Browns, before a massive crowd of 84,213. The New York team won handily, 33-6, in what later was called "the perfect game." The Giants came as close as a pro football team can come to making no mistakes.

From the Frank Gifford standpoint, the remarkable part was that he did not get into the game until it was won, well won. He was in perfect health and there he stood at the sidelines, his hands in the pockets of the blue warm-up jacket, his eyes staring at Y. A. Tittle, as the bald Giant quarterback directed the potent offensive unit up and down the field.

Although Allie Sherman, the coach, tried to duck

the issue, Gifford had simply been passed over in favor of someone else, namely Aaron Thomas, for the flanker-back position. The Giants had so many good receivers that season that all of a sudden there was no room for Gifford in the starting lineup.

Del Shofner, an all-league performer, was at split end; Joe Walton at tight end; Thomas, for this game at least, on the flank, plus Gifford.

Gifford was a little sullen about it, as well he might have been. Not since his sophomore year at Bakersfield High had he been cast in the role of a substitute. Brief note was made of Gifford's new status in the press but no one paid much attention because the Giants were collectively flying high, headed for their third straight eastern division championship.

Walton came down with a minor injury for the next game and Thomas moved to tight end with Gifford restored to the flank. Sherman, taking cognizance of Gifford's injured feelings, judiciously juggled his receiving corps the rest of the season.

After the final game, in which Gifford made his great catch against Pittsburgh, Sherman tried to make it up to Frank and chose an easy whipping boy—the press. Said Allie, "That guy they were burying not long ago made it great for us, didn't he?" Inasmuch as Sherman, not "they," had turned the first spade of earth, it was hard to believe that Gifford paid much attention to the remark.

Although he was thereafter a regular to the end of his playing days with the Giants, which came at the conclusion of the following season, Gifford received a small message that afternoon when he stood on the sidelines at Cleveland. The end was coming, the time when he would have to give up the game he loved.

When he was learning his new position, flankerback rather than halfback, at the Giants' training camp in Fairfield, Connecticut, during July of 1962, Gifford explained to Jimmy Cannon of the New York *Journal American* another motive for his return. "I'll be honest with you," he said. "It's sort of an ego thing. The good ones like it. Hell, I get more excitement in one day playing football than most people get in a lifetime."

His comeback had not been easy. Although Gifford had on many occasions been flanked to the right side when he was the left halfback in the old Lombardi offense, most of the time he had run pass patterns out to the left side. As a full-time flanker he found at first that he had a hard time holding on to the football. In a preseason game against Philadelphia he dropped three passes. For Gifford that was unheard of. "I never felt lower," he said. "The ball seems to spin differently on the right side. It hits the hands with an unfamiliar feel."

Because Kyle Rote had retired, Sherman needed Gifford as a wide receiver and he stuck with the old hero, knowing full well that Frank would master his new role. He did and one who helped was a brilliant cornerback, Erich Barnes. He played opposite Gifford in all the practice pass drills. They enjoyed beating one another, and in the process these two fine athletes enhanced one another's skills.

The Giants blazed through the 1962 season, winning 10 out of 12 games. Gifford did very well, catching 39 passes for 796 yards and seven touchdowns. Shofner was the team leader with 53.

The Green Bay Packers were the Giants' opponents in the championship game played at Yankee Stadium on a raw, cold day with a gale blowing. The wind was so strong that Tittle's passes failed to hold their trajectory and the Giants, now a passing team, could not do without this weapon. "The ball would be coming toward me," said Gifford, "and then all of a sudden it would take off. It sailed."

The Packers won a bitter, hard-fought game, 16-7.

The 1963 season saw more of the same. The Giants won 11 out of 14 games and scored 448 points, the second highest total in league history. Gifford's contribution was 42 receptions for 657 yards and seven touchdowns. Shofner again was the team leader with 64 receptions.

The opponent in the championship game this time was the Chicago Bears, a team with a defense that had given up an average of only 10 points per game. The Bears gave the Giants just 10 and scored 14 themselves. Tittle injured his knee in the second period and was never right thereafter. Gifford caught three passes, one for a touchdown, and obviously had his defender, Bennie McRae, intimidated. But the ball did not come to him often enough.

A sharp reversal in the Giants' fortunes took place in 1964. Sherman seemed dissatisfied with merely winning. As a super-sensitive man he paid attention rather than ignore comments that suggested he had won three division titles with a team he had largely inherited from a prior coaching regime. So Allie set out to build his own team. He began by trading away Sam Huff, which was logical enough, except the Giants had no adequate replacement for him.

The team was growing old in a lot of places at once and the erosion set in quickly. The 1964 club won only two games and finished dead last in the east.

It was interesting to watch Gifford, however. He knew it was his last season and even though the team was in chaos he never quit.

Tittle did not take kindly to misfortune and the old quarterback lost a lot of his poise. Toward the end of the dismal season a rookie from Cornell named Gary Wood was playing quarterback. Wood, 5 feet 10, could not see his receivers so well and he went looking for Gifford most often. "I know I just got here," said Wood. "But Gifford has to be one of the best receivers in the game. I just wish I could get the ball to him more often."

On March 19, 1965, Frank Gifford announced his second and, as he put it, "final" retirement as a player. A fat, new contract with CBS as a sports telecaster was also revealed as a part of the ceremonies held in Toots Shor's new restaurant.

Jack Mara, the team president, who was to die of cancer that June, said it well: "The Giants in their 40 years have had many outstanding players. Once in a long while one comes along who stands out above the others. Frank Gifford was such a one. He was a great credit to us both on and off the field. Our loss is CBS's gain."

Gifford thanked a lot of people but specifically the Mara family who had been such friends as well as considerate employers. In an interview later, he was asked about the one play that stood out in his long Giant career. He went for the big catch against the Steelers in the final game of the 1963 season, the difficult catch that opened the way to a New York victory and another division title.

"It was probably the best I've ever made," he said. "Certainly the most important. All I was trying to do was bat the ball up in the air. I didn't think it would stick in my hand."

It was said of Gifford, in looking backwards, that he brought to pro football unusual qualities beyond his mere physical skills. "Half the time," someone said, "Gifford went out of his way to convince the football crowd he was not an egghead, the other half to prove to himself he was not a numbskull."

Many years ago, when he was in his prime, Gifford once said, "When I finish football, we hope to go off to Europe to ski in winter, spend lots of time in Italy, sip good wine, bask in the sun, write a book, and think back on the days when Gifford was a halfback for the New York Giants."

He has yet to do this.

EPILOGUE

The first time I ever met Frank Gifford was in early September of 1959, a couple of weeks before the season opened, a season that was to be a brilliant one for the Giants.

Our initial confrontation occurred under rather strained circumstances. The team was at Bear Mountain State Park, having left the training camp at Winooski in Vermont. It was "picture day," an afternoon set aside for the newspaper, magazine and television photographers up from New York so that they could take many posed, and for the most part phony, pictures of the Giants in their new, clean blue uniforms.

I was then in my third year of the five I spent working for the New York *Herald Tribune* as a sportswriter. My sports editor, the late Stanley Woodward, held a low opinion of pro football and perhaps that is why he had consented the day before to my request to be assigned to cover the Giants for the paper.

I had been around football for a long time, covering college football (mostly the Ivy League) for the *Herald Tribune* and earlier for the New York *World-Telegram & Sun,* my first employer in New York back in 1949. One of the side benefits of belonging to the sports staff of a metropolitan paper in those days was free tickets to the pro football games. Since the sport had no special popularity, the Giants' management was liberal in dispensing complimentary tickets. I had a pair in the upper deck of the Polo Grounds on the 50-yard line and I seldom missed a home game. Often there were plenty of empty seats around me.

In those early years we hustled to get to the game on time to see if Emlen Tunnell might run the kick-off back for a touchdown. Tunnell's kick-off and punt returns were the most exciting part of teams that lacked distinction, except occasionally on defense.

So I was a Giant fan, and a reasonably knowledgeable one, when the task of covering the team for the *Herald Tribune* became open. I bullied Woodward into giving me the assignment.

I arrived at Bear Mountain with scant knowledge of Jim Lee Howell, the coach, and unacquainted with the players who were more like heroes to me than subjects to write about. I was 35 years old and reticent, if not shy.

The day happened to be important to Gifford and a unique one for him because there were overtones of failure in the air. Failure was something that seldom if ever had occurred to Frank Gifford and he had no special humility in handling it. At least that is what I thought when I finished a stiff, somewhat uninformative interview with him.

Gifford had decided in the months between seasons that he wanted to become a quarterback, a T-formation quarterback to replace or at least supplement his old friend, Charley Conerly.

He had two motives. First, he thought he could help the team. Defenses had come to contain the Giants' offense and the club found it harder and harder to move the ball and score points. Conerly, by then aging, if not aged at 38, was a passing quarterback. No one expected him to run with the football and their expectations were correct. When Charley was in a jam he threw the ball away.

Gifford reasoned that the time was ripe to add the running element to the quarterback position. He suspected he could run well enough from quarterback to open up the Giants' offense. Besides he had been a T quarterback briefly in high school and college, and he was a good college passer from tailback in the single wing.

The other motive was personal. Gifford knew that pro quarterbacks seemed to go on forever. If he could effect the position shift his playing career might be extended by several seasons. He was then 29, and 29-year-old running backs are old.

Gifford wrote Howell a letter in late June. "Dear Jim Lee: I know this may sound like a strange request, but I certainly hope you will give it consideration. To come right to the point, I would like to play quarterback for the Giants. Charley Conerly is my best friend and he has done a wonderful job for us over the years. But I think the time has come when our club needs a quarterback who can run as well as pass. I think I'm that man. The defenses have been stacking up against Charley because they know he doesn't run the ball. This has hurt his passing—and our entire offense."

Howell was skeptical and somewhat shocked. Because of Conerly's age the team was looking for a possible replacement. But Gifford?

A skeptical Howell agreed to the experiment. It seemed expedient to acquiesce to this fine athlete's request. If the experiment did not work, Gifford would still be the team's left halfback.

In training camp, Gifford did fairly well. He had one outstanding half in the first preseason game against the Eagles but was less impressive in the next two contests. There was too little opportunity to test him and to train him because the start of the season was imminent and others needed work. Conerly, typically noncommittal about Gifford's move, had to get ready. Don Heinrich was still on the scene and the team's touted new rookie, Lee Grosscup from Utah, had to be inspected.

What ended the Gifford experiment once and for all was the sudden availability of George Shaw, the player who had been the regular quarterback for the Baltimore Colts until John Unitas took his job away in 1956. The Giants of the time thought Shaw was a lot better than he turned out to be and they quickly made the trade, believing they had Conerly's successor. The cost was high, a first and a second draft choice. Shaw was gone by the start of the 1961 season.

With four quarterbacks—Conerly, Heinrich, Shaw and Grosscup—on hand, Gifford went back to left halfback. The day of his announced return was the Bear Mountain day. The prideful Gifford was not about to admit that he could not make it as a quarterback. Circumstances merely prevented the continuation of his changeover, he explained coolly to me and several other reporters.

I had the feeling as he dismissed me that he was wondering who this new kid on the block might be. Rookie writers as well as rookie players go through a kind of indoctrination, a mild hazing. I wrote the games up as I saw them that year—it was a championship season for the Giants—and spoke to next to no one except the coaches. They were more or less obliged to keep the press informed.

My relationship with Gifford was not enhanced the next season, hardly a great one for the Giants. The team won six games, lost four and tied two, dropping to third place in the East as the Eagles finished first. The New York offense slowed to a halt, as Conerly was injured part of the time. It seemed to me that Gifford had to be included in the general demise and I had the temerity to suggest in print that perhaps the great one had lost a step of speed because the holes now seemed to close before he got through them.

Frank made it clear he did not care for any such suggestion and perhaps that was when he bestowed on me, partly in jest, the sobriquet "Poison Pen."

"Here comes Poison Pen," he might say, albeit with a smile.

The matter became purely academic following the game against Philadelphia when Gifford sustained his concussion. He was not to play again until 1962 and then it was as a flanker rather than a running back.

Our relationship improved a lot when he came back and especially after Maxine Gifford and my wife became friends in the summer of 1963. It just so happened that my home was in Southport, Connecticut, a town adjacent to Fairfield where the Giants trained in the summer.

A friend of mine, Chester J. LaRoche, had four of the players to his house one evening for what was an informal yet elegant dinner. The players were Del Shofner, Phil King, Hugh McElhenny and Gifford with his wife. Although LaRoche was an avid football man and the longtime president of the National Football Foundation, he barely knew these athletes and I suppose I was invited to help serve as a social bridge.

We proceeded through dinner smoothly even though one of the players was mighty suspicious about the finger bowl placed before him. I suspected he thought it might be another martini. After dinner I had the good sense to let the athletes enjoy coffee and a cigar with the host, who did want to get to know them. His experience had been confined to college players, mostly from his alma mater, Yale.

So I remained with the ladies for about an hour and then decided to move to the den and see how the boys were making out. I found LaRoche, an idealist, sitting silently in a deep chair and listening. He appeared to be rather stunned and I soon realized why. The conversation was not about football but how much money one could make through endorsements and various other moonlighting opportunities outside of the game. It was avaricious, unromantic talk and since Gifford was far the busiest in this field many of the questions were directed to him. "How much do you get from Jantzen, Frank?"

As I left that evening LaRoche put his arm around my shoulder and said, "Well, they certainly are different, Bill."

After that the Giffords and the Wallaces socialized occasionally. One especially memorable evening followed the Sunday on which Pete Rozelle ordered the National Football League's scheduled games to go on even though President Kennedy was to be buried the next day.

The Cardinals had beaten the Giants at Yankee Stadium and that evening we assembled in the Giffords' small apartment in The Croydon Hotel on East 86th Street. Jack Ruby had shot Lee Oswald that afternoon and we watched the reruns and drank. Peggy and Hugh McElhenny, the Giants' halfback, were there. Later the six of us wandered around the city until McElhenny's sore leg stiffened up on him. It was quite unreal.

By this time, I decided, Gifford had come to trust me and to consider me to be something more than another nosey reporter. I found him to be a relaxed, easy man, acute and equipped with a gentle needle to go with his dry humor. He was good company.

The next summer the Giffords again rented a cottage on the beach in Fairfield for the training camp period. Because the boys, Jeffrey and Kyle, and Vicky, their daughter, liked the beach, it made no difference that their cottage was a sort of shack.

It was 1964, the year that everything went out of the Giants. The balloon came down. The team won two games, lost ten, tied two, for the poorest record in the league. A lot of the players were older and had become worn down. Young new players in other cities like Cleveland and Dallas became highly competitive. The Browns and the Cowboys passed the Giants by.

Gifford apparently had a sense of impending doom as we talked one evening. The two couples went down to my beach for a swim and dinner at the end of one of those days in which the temperature and the humidity had joined in the 90's.

I had been to New Jersey to cover a tennis tournament and was full of self-pity by the time I had driven home. I complained to Gifford about what a hot, difficult day I had.

"Well, what do you think we were doing today?" he asked contemptuously. "Double workout, morning and afternoon. Four guys passed out in the afternoon." That shut me up.

Because the Giants had won three eastern division titles in a row, I thought they would go on and on with Y. A. Tittle throwing dozens of touchdown passes as he had in the past, to make up for whatever other deficiencies might arise.

Gifford had his doubts and he expressed them, simply

and briefly. I did not push him. I thought of him as a friend by now and there was no reporter in me. Besides, the working day had passed and there was cool peace in the evening at the beach.

Frank and my wife went for a swim in the club pool while Maxine—Max that is—and I talked. Then the Giffords went home in the new Mustang that Frank had bought for his wife.

I wondered later if that scene was real. It seemed so at the time. Gifford was six years younger than I but our wives were of the same age and so were our children. Yet he was a professional football player and I was more or less a commuter. On that score there should have been a disassociation. Yet there was none. There never again would be for me a time like that, a time in which a player—one of my journalistic subjects—would be someone I regarded as a contemporary in life as well as a friend. I knew by the following year that an era had ended.

The next summer Gifford came to Fairfield only once or twice and his role was different. He was a television broadcaster covering the team for WCBS-TV in New York. The Giants had a number of new young players that summer, most of them rookies, and Gifford felt as distant from them as I did. At any rate he asked me quietly and unobtrusively which player was which. I considered that to be a compliment, a sign of trust.

I treasure few pictures. One shows Tittle in a business suit holding a Giant helmet and a jersey while being held aloft by Frank Gifford and Rosey Brown. It was taken at the luncheon in the winter of 1965 when Tittle announced his retirement as a player. These were three fairly sensational athletes, the likes of whom I do not expect to see together again on any Giant team.

An autograph? Because there is no need, I've never asked Gifford for one and I never will. Similarly, he has never asked me for mine.

THE GOLDEN YEAR SERIES

The Golden Year Series consists of books devoted to the most spectacular year in the careers of America's outstanding athletic figures. In addition to Frank Gifford, other sports greats who will be featured are: Joe DiMaggio, Jim Brown, Ted Williams, Jack Dempsey, Gordie Howe, Arnold Palmer, and more.